The Films of Joseph Losey examines the career of the expatriate director through a close analysis of five of his most important and challenging films. When his leftist politics made him a target of the House Committee on Un-American Activities in 1951, the blacklisted Losey left the United States and continued his film career in England. Concerned mainly with the use and abuse of power inherent in intimate relationships, Losey also explored these issues as manifested in institutions and social classes. His finest films attack the injustices and hypocrisy rooted in the privileges of the English class system and frequently depict the moral failure of characters who betray their best instincts. *The Films of Joseph Losey* also discusses Losey's close working relationship with playwright-screenwriter Harold Pinter and actor Dirk Bogarde, his experimental form of storytelling, the psychological complexity of characters acting as narrators of their own stories, and the intricate handling of time in the structure of his films. Close studies of *King and Country, The Servant, Accident, The Go-Between,* and *The Romantic Englishwoman* confirm Losey's stature as a director of powerful and compelling films of both moral importance and great formal complexity.

The Films of Joseph Losey

CAMBRIDGE FILM CLASSICS

General Editor: Raymond Carney, Boston University

Other books in the series:

Peter Bondanella, *The Films of Roberto Rossellini*
Sam B. Girgus, *The Films of Woody Allen*
Robert Phillip Kolker and Peter Beicken, *The Films of Wim Wenders*
Scott MacDonald, *Avant-Garde Film*
James Naremore, *The Films of Vincente Minnelli*
Scott Simmon, *The Films of D. W. Griffith*
David Sterritt, *The Films of Alfred Hitchcock*
Maurice Yacowar, *The Films of Paul Morrissey*

The Films of
Joseph Losey

JAMES PALMER
University of Colorado, Boulder

MICHAEL RILEY
Claremont McKenna College

CAMBRIDGE
UNIVERSITY PRESS

Published by the Press Syndicate of the University of Cambridge
The Pitt Building, Trumpington Street, Cambridge CB2 1RP
40 West 20th Street, New York, NY 10011-4211, USA
10 Stamford Road, Oakleigh, Victoria 3166, Australia

First published 1993

Printed in the United States of America

Library of Congress Cataloging-in-Publication Data
Palmer, James, 1940–
The films of Joseph Losey / James Palmer, Michael Riley.
p.   cm. – (Cambridge film classics)
Filmography: p.
Includes bibliographical references and index.
ISBN 0-521-38386-2 (hc). – ISBN 0-521-38780-9 (pb)
1. Losey, Joseph – Criticism and interpretation.   1. Riley,
Michael, 1935–   . II. Title. III. Series.
PN1998.3.L68P35   1993
791.43'0233'092 – dc20   92-37480
                                          CIP

A catalog record for this book is available from the British Library.

ISBN 0-521-38386-2 hardback
ISBN 0-521-38780-9 paperback

To Sue, Sydney, and Sarah — without whom
even movies are meaningless

J.P.

To French Fogle and the memory of Fred Mulhauser
and Beverle Houston — whose wise counsel and generous
friendship made a great difference

M.R.

Contents

Acknowledgments

Several institutions and numerous friends and colleagues made valuable contributions to this book. We thank Madeline Matz of the Library of Congress, Larry Gordon of Arlington Properties, and the UCLA Film Archive for making it possible for us to view films that were otherwise unavailable. The staff of the Center for Motion Picture Study at the Academy of Motion Picture Arts and Sciences was always helpful. So, too, Scott Woodland and his staff at Boulder's Video Station, surely one of the country's premier video stores, were unfailingly expert, cheerful, and patient.

We are especially grateful to those who read and commented on various drafts of the manuscript. Les Brill and Langdon Elsbree read it in its entirety with characteristic rigor and sympathetic interest. Cathy Comstock, Paul Gordon, Marian Keane, Susan Linville, and Nick Warner read various chapters and offered comments that helped us sharpen our argument. The late Beverle Houston read an early version of the chapter on *Accident* and made valuable suggestions with her usual critical insight and generosity. In England Brian Davis helped with details in the discussion of *King and Country*, and David Caute, Joseph Losey's biographer, kindly offered astute comments and checked the accuracy of the biographical passages and the filmography. We also thank Mary Losey Field for her assistance and good wishes.

We are grateful to Rubin Rabinovitz and Bryan Bach for being generous with their time and computer expertise. In Boulder Hazel Barnes, Virgil Grillo, and Nancy Hill have offered steadfast support over the years, as has Bob Fossum in Claremont. Special thanks are due Bruce Kawin for originally suggesting this project. Our thanks also to Beatrice Rehl of Cambridge University Press and Raymond Carney, general editor of Cambridge Film

Classics, for their enthusiasm and support, and to Robert Racine and Mary Racine for their meticulous editing.

Several of the ideas in this book profited from the keen questions and comments of students in a course on film narrative at Claremont McKenna College. Particular acknowledgment is due Lucia Chapelle, Hilly Hicks, Broderick Miller, Peter Otte, and Kevin Walder.

For permission to reproduce frame enlargements we thank British Home Entertainment (*King and Country*), Daniel Angel and Dial Trading Limited (*The Romantic Englishwoman*), and Weintraub Entertainment Limited (*The Servant, Accident,* and *The Go-Between*). Our thanks to the editor of *College Literature* and the CWRU Film Society for permission to use previously published material. Portions of Chapter 3 appeared as " 'An Extension of Reality': Setting as Theme in *The Servant*," *Mise-en-Scène* 2 (1980), and of Chapter 5 as "Time and Memory in *The Go-Between*," *College Literature* 3 (1978).

We are also grateful to Claremont McKenna College and the University of Colorado for grants to help defray the cost of obtaining permissions and frame enlargements.

I

"Pictures of Provocation"

The expatriate American director Joseph Losey (1909–84) claimed his place among important filmmakers with such rich films as *The Servant* (1963), *King and Country* (1964), *Accident* (1967), *The Go-Between* (1971), and *The Romantic Englishwoman* (1975). His reputation, however, remains unjustifiably problematic. For some he is an allegorist detached from his characters, for others principally a stylist with a penchant for the gothic. Admittedly the body of his work includes both great achievements and failed aspirations; masterful films stand amid misbegotten efforts such as *Modesty Blaise* (1966) and *Boom!* (1968). Moreover, critics have disagreed radically about the very nature and characteristics of his work. The French critic Gilles Jacob, for example, writes of Losey's "unshakable faith in human nature" (1966, 64), whereas Foster Hirsch concludes that the "world-view" in his films is "essentially negative, their sense of the possibilities of human nature and society deeply pessimistic" (1980, 220). The effort to see Losey's achievement whole has been further complicated by the drama of his personal history and the several ways of dividing his filmmaking career. After only five feature films in the United States, in the years 1948–51, he was blacklisted and moved to England, never making another film in his own country although he expressed the desire to do so and, on at least one occasion, nearly succeeded. Given the blacklist and Losey's subsequent exile, the most obvious division of his films is between those produced in Hollywood and those after. But the films he made after Hollywood can also be divided between the English and the European, and the three films he made from screenplays by Harold Pinter can be distinguished from his other English films made both before and after their collaboration. Despite these complications and the range of critical opinions, an overview of Losey's films reveals a major filmmaker profoundly committed to his art, always growing in his command of his medium, willing to take risks that would have daunted a lesser artist, and at his best the director of an impressive number of exhilarating and complex narrative films.

Losey's position as an expatriate who made films in several countries led to his own amused comment in an interview in *American Film* that "there's quite a good deal of confusion in the world as to what I am, in terms of a director. The French now think I'm English. A lot of the English think I'm English. The Italians think I'm French.... Anyway, it's unimportant, isn't it? I wanted to make some pictures because I think that I have a certain distance that has made it possible for me to comment on certain European societies and situations in ways that perhaps otherwise I couldn't have done" (1980, 59–60). Losey's outsider status worked both for and against him; he was "at home" everywhere and nowhere. As he suggested, he could bring the fresh perspective of a cultural outsider to conflicts arising from the class system in England or, in a late film like *La Truite* (1982), from the sexual mores of contemporary France. But his status as an independent director also meant continual struggles to get financing for his various projects (more than sixty aborted projects, not to mention the loss of the final editing rights on *Eve* [1962], a film the producers recut and shortened by some forty minutes, thus destroying Losey's original conception of "a film which I think came as close to being a great film as I had ever achieved" [Ciment 1985, 222]). His disappointment with *Eve,* however, was followed by the great success of the first of his three extraordinary films with Harold Pinter, *The Servant,* which marked a turning point in his career.

As his many interviews reveal, Losey was an artist who thought long and deeply about his work, a man of exceptional candor, as ready to judge some of his films harshly as to express his pleasure in others. (He liked *The Prowler* [1951], *The Servant,* and *Accident,* for instance, but of *The Gypsy and the Gentleman* [1958], he confessed with some dismay, "I think it's largely a piece of junk, and I'd just as soon nobody saw it again" [Gow 1971, 39].) He was also generous in his praise of his collaborators: designers John Hubley, Alexandre Trauner, and especially Richard MacDonald, with whom he often worked and who, in Losey's words, "contributed genius"; writers Evan Jones, Alun Owen, David Mercer, Tennessee Williams, and of course Pinter; cinematographer Gerry Fisher; editors Reginald Beck and Reginald Mills; actors such as Stanley Baker, who had some of his best roles (*Blind Date* [1959], *The Criminal* [1960], and *Accident*) in Losey's films, and preeminently Dirk Bogarde, whose five films with Losey, including three to be discussed in this book, were instrumental in transforming a popular leading man in England into one of the finest screen actors in the

2

world. Losey's expressed admiration for these and other fellow artists was returned in the form of repeated collaborations, evidence of a bond of sympathy and trust that he referred to more than once and that obviously gratified him deeply.

In an art-industry beset by a persistent conflict between artistic aspirations and commercial timidity, by a disheartening number of projects planned but unfulfilled, Losey's frustrations with producers, financiers, and distributors both in the United States and abroad were perhaps not greater than those of other major filmmakers. The topic is a sad commonplace in the careers of most of his peers. But in light of his considerable achievements, Losey's unrealized hopes for films based on Thomas Hardy's *The Mayor of Casterbridge,* Joseph Conrad's *Nostromo,* and most of all, with Harold Pinter, Marcel Proust's *A la recherche du temps perdu* further suggest the imposing range of his interests and the high ambition of his artistry. One can only lament that Losey never had the chance to make these and other films he planned. Many of the films that he did make, however – those we discuss and others we have reluctantly excluded for reasons of space – linger in the memory and compel an admiration that belongs only to an artist of the first rank. More importantly, as this book will argue, several of Losey's finest films challenge and expand one's understanding of film as a narrative medium in their bold exploration of narration as an informing principle of cinematic form and expression.

At present, the most detailed account of Losey's life and the best source for biographical information is Michel Ciment's *Conversations with Losey* (1985), which is based on a series of interviews that begins with a discussion of Losey's early years and continues through his comments on *La Truite,* his next to last film.[1] The book concludes with an afterword by his widow Patricia Losey, who collaborated closely with him over a number of years and who adapted Nell Dunn's stage play for his last film, *Steaming* (1985). Losey's candor, his views of his professional frustrations, his self-criticism, his generosity toward his collaborators, his insecurities, his commitment to his art – all come through with clarity and sometimes wry wit in his extended talks with Ciment. From these interviews, one has an overview not only of the period of his greatest successes, but also of his formative years, his education, his politics, and his apprenticeship in the world of theater and film.

Losey's Midwest background helped both to define him and to provide a culture against which he could rebel. Born in La Crosse, Wisconsin, to parents of English, Dutch, and German extraction, he recalled to Ciment his early memories of big houses, large family gatherings, and an Aunt Mary whose "Proustian" house full of Japanese prints and porcelain from around the world provided hospitality for touring celebrities such as Ford Madox Ford, Mark Twain, and Hamlin Garland. Losey also commented on his Episcopalian training, his mother's snobbishness, and the pervasive preju-dices (anti-Catholic, anti-Semitic, anti-Norwegian) of a small-town com-munity. When he was sixteen, his father died suddenly of peritonitis; he recalled his subsequent relationship with his mother as difficult and distant, and he was to see her infrequently after he left Wisconsin for Dartmouth College in 1925. In his senior year at Dartmouth Losey broke his back in a freak theater accident. A year in the hospital, which he spent reading and studying, led him to change from medical studies ("a completely false vo-cation that I'd imposed on myself") to theater and English literature; after graduation, he completed a masters degree in English at Harvard in 1930. "The back thing was a blessing in disguise," he told Ciment, "as the black list was a blessing in disguise. The catastrophies in my life seemed to have always worked out for my benefit" (1985, 22).

In 1931 and again in 1935 Losey traveled to Europe. On the latter trip he visited Russia, where he met Vsevolod Meyerhold, the actor and avant-garde theater director, and even directed an English-language production of Clifford Odets's *Waiting for Lefty* in Moscow. He briefly thought of staying in Russia, but was talked out of the idea by a member of the Politburo who, he later said with characteristic candor, "was really like a breath of fresh air because he cut through all of my nonsense, my idealistic nonsense" (Ciment 1985, 41). In the thirties, Losey became a Marxist, and later in Hollywood he joined the Communist party, a move that was to have a great and disturbing impact on his life. Living in New York City throughout the thirties, he first wrote theater reviews, then worked as a stage manager, and eventually directed plays, working with such writers as Sinclair Lewis and Maxwell Anderson. His New York experience was a blend of theater, pol-itics, and film that led him to work for such politically oriented groups as *The Living Newspaper*, the Federal Theater, the Political Cabaret, and even-tually to begin making educational and documentary films. When the war broke out, Losey worked for the United War Relief and then volunteered for the Air Corps, but a dossier of his political activities thwarted his en-listment, and he spent the better part of a year working in radio for NBC. Ironically, before the war ended, he was drafted into the army and ended up making films in the Signal Corps.

After the war, Losey worked for MGM, directing a short film, *A Gun in*

His Hand (1945), that received an Academy Award nomination. His chance to direct his first Hollywood feature came when Dore Schary, executive producer at RKO, asked him to make *The Boy with Green Hair* with producer Adrian Scott. But when Scott was subpoenaed in 1947 to appear before the House Committee on Un-American Activities, production plans for the film were suspended. Meanwhile Losey helped stage a large rally at the Shrine Auditorium in Los Angeles for the defenders of the Hollywood Nineteen (before the Nineteen became the Hollywood Ten), and soon after this event, he mounted a celebrated stage production of his close friend Bertolt Brecht's *Galileo*, starring Charles Laughton, which was presented in Los Angeles just prior to Brecht's appearance before the HUAC and subsequent hurried departure for Europe. A few months later the production was also staged in New York. Despite these highly visible public activities, Losey somehow survived the first round of blacklisting. Dore Schary again asked him to direct *The Boy with Green Hair,* but of course without Scott as producer. (Schary was himself fired by RKO's owner, Howard Hughes, before *The Boy with Green Hair* [1948] was completed.) This antiracist, pro-peace allegory or fable, which remains popular today, was attacked as a "red" film, a film that, according to Losey, "Hughes tried his best to change"; failing that, Hughes threatened him with a message about his contract: " 'You'll stay here for seven years and you'll never work' " (Ciment 1985, 82). Finally, his friendship with Brecht, his defense of Adrian Scott, his sponsorship of composer Hans Eisler (brother of Gerhardt Eisler, the head of the Communist party in East Germany), and his own party membership all made him vulnerable when the HUAC investigations were revived in 1951.

Losey's blacklisting has been much commented on by himself and others, and it certainly played a crucial role in the direction his career was to take. Without going into great detail, any summary of his attitudes about the blacklisting – about the witch-hunting, the scapegoating, and the betrayal by friends and colleagues – reveals one essential thing, and that is Losey's concern for maintaining a sense of personal integrity both during and after the blacklisting era. As he commented in a radio interview later:

> There is the terrible problem – how to be honest, as honest as one can. How not to betray, or seem to betray... what one believed and did in extreme youth – whether in the 1930's or during the war or in the post-war period. I don't think anyone in his right mind wants to say "I didn't do this, I didn't stand for this, or I stood for this because I was a dupe," or whatever the escape-hatches may be. Because those

attitudes or those points of view – no matter how limited they might have been or whatever caused them at the time – they are what one has developed from. They are part of what one is. And if you deny them, you do yourself and everyone else a great disservice, because then you obscure instead of clarifying. ("Speak, Think, Stand Up" 1970, 60)

In Victor Navasky's *Naming Names,* Losey gives a fascinating account of the events surrounding his being named a Communist, and of his betrayer who some years later offered him an attractive film project that he turned down (1980, 357–59). Controversy marked Losey's film career from its inception, and the political turmoil of the late forties and early fifties in America eventually turned him from a Hollywood director into an expatriate director. Ironically, as Losey told Gene Phillips: "In a way my being black-listed was one of the best things that ever happened to me because it forced me to go to Europe to continue my career as a film maker. Otherwise I might have stayed on in Hollywood merely making money instead of making pictures I want to make. What could be worse than that?" (1976, 34–5).

Speaking about the didactic qualities of his first two Hollywood features, *The Boy with Green Hair* and *The Lawless* (1950), Losey succinctly put into perspective the kind of films he made not only in the United States, but for his first several years in England:

They were what is called "message" pictures. And they were made by a man – me – and other men and women, who thought we knew the answers or thought we could find answers. I stopped somewhere along the line – I guess at *Eve* maybe – making that kind of picture, and have been much more interested in making pictures of provocation: that is, opening up the mind so people have to examine situations and attitudes and come to their own conclusions. (Ciment 1985, 97)

Interestingly, for a few critics the early melodramas in Hollywood are Losey's finest. The French critic Pierre Rissient, for example, argues in his book *Losey* (1966) that the American films are his best, simple, unpretentious, and the more successful for these traits. But Losey himself never concurred in this assessment. With typical frankness he told Ciment that *The Boy with Green Hair* "certainly is obviously a first film" (1985, 88). He was dissatisfied with the studio settings (they seemed unrealistic to Losey, who knew from his own experience what small towns were like and who would have preferred location shooting) and frustrated in trying to deal with the film's mix of fantasy and reality, notably in the war orphan scene that was shot

6

in a studio-built glade and even in the charming song and dance fantasy with Pat O'Brien and veteran vaudevillean Walter Catleff. Losey also felt that the film was compromised by mixing a pro-peace message into what was "basically an allegory about racism" (Milne 1968, 66). Similarly, although he liked *The Lawless,* Losey told Milne that the film was "very primitive as a piece of work" (1968, 83), one that, as he said to James Leahy, "belongs to a very early period of thinking for me.... I was still trying to get out of my system, I suppose, some of the things which were very much a part of me in the thirties and early forties" (1967, 34–5).

Despite Losey's perceptive criticism of his early films, this stage in his career reveals something more than merely a politically committed neophyte director learning his craft. For instance, *The Boy with Green Hair,* quite apart from its troubled production history, merits attention not just as the first feature of a filmmaker who went on to a distinguished career, but as a film that demonstrates its director's already considerable strengths. Whatever its limits, the film remains not just a well-meaning if obvious work of earnest social criticism, but a promising film of charm and sensitivity, marked by excellent performances by Pat O'Brien, Robert Ryan, and especially the twelve-year-old Dean Stockwell. Indeed Losey's skill with actors would be remarked on by many performers who worked with him subsequently. The film contains affecting scenes of prejudice and betrayal by the boy's peers and the community's leaders. The boy's green hair, more effective as a symbol of his individuality, his "color" difference, than as a symbol of renewal or peace, is, with the townspeople's approval, cut off in the barbershop scene that is simultaneously poignant and discomfiting. Adults and children alike witness the shaving of the boy's head, revealing the power of their conformist thinking and, ironically, compromising their own individuality as well. Thus, in his first film Losey expressed a theme that he would turn to again and again – the cowardly and ultimately hypocritical responses of characters confronting ethical dilemmas in which they betray themselves as well as others.

Although Losey ascribed to *The Prowler,* his third film, "a kind of Hollywood polish which I don't admire and don't strive for," he also counted it "a very smooth picture ... which really doesn't date" (Ciment 1985, 104). Certainly, of his early films it is the one that best suggests the directions his mature work would take. Written by Hugo Butler and Dalton Trumbo, both of whom were to be blacklisted (Trumbo was uncredited because he had already been identified as one of the Hollywood Ten), *The Prowler* is an effective film noir about a morally adrift policeman who contrives to murder a beautiful woman's older husband (allegedly mistaking him for a

7

prowler) in order to get the woman and her money for himself. If the plot seems conventional film noir fare for the early fifties, Losey's handling of the material pushes against the somewhat overworked patterns of the genre. The character of the wife Susan (Evelyn Keyes), for instance, reverses the usual femme fatale. Unlike the wife in *Double Indemnity,* who betrays her lover after luring him into murdering her husband, Susan is the one manipulated. She responds ambivalently to Garwood (Van Heflin), the policeman who becomes her lover, one minute defending her husband and rejecting Garwood's advances and the next desperate in her desire for him. An easy mark for the hypocritical cop, she becomes Garwood's unknowing accomplice, playing her role perfectly because she is unaware of his schemes. Materialistic and manipulative, Garwood is a predator who will not be deterred. Although the initial prowler is never seen (the opening camera shot constitutes the viewer's voyeuristic gaze and Susan's discovery of our look), Garwood quickly becomes the prowling intruder. His successful schemes founded on deceiving others are based on self-deception as well. But however crudely ambitious, Garwood is something more than a cardboard character. Both calculating and naive, crass and genuinely confused by his conflicting values that make him see Susan as his ticket to the good life and his only hope for a relationship that will break through his loneliness, Garwood is an alternately repellent and pathetic victim of his self-destructive action. In his moral and psychological isolation, he seems oddly to pursue loneliness even as he tries to live out his dream.

Significantly, in its provocative study of the policeman, *The Prowler* anticipates two elements that will appear with increasing frequency in Losey's films – his complex use of physical settings as an element of characterization, and the motif of the intruder. The married couple's large and somewhat vulgar house so impressive to the envious policeman; the motel that he buys with the money gained from his murder of the husband and marriage to the unwitting widow; and the stark desert ghost town in which his corrupt dream comes to an end – all reveal the hapless murderer's character and his perverse enactment of an American success story. Like so many of Losey's characters, Garwood is not just a loner but an intruder, an outsider who enters a closed social world only to disrupt or subvert that world or be destroyed by it. In Garwood's case, both of these things happen. Indeed, in many respects he is a quintessential Losey character – competitive, hypocritical, manipulative, sexually opportunistic, internally divided, and self-destructive. Garwood is the progenitor of Barrett in *The Servant,* Stephen in *Accident,* and Robert Klein in *Mr. Klein* (1976), a man whose temporary success in fulfilling his dream ultimately damns him.

With his Hollywood career brought to a close by the HUAC investigations and the resulting blacklisting of directors, writers, and actors on the political left, Losey directed in Italy in 1952 the first film to be made abroad by a blacklisted artist (*Stranger on the Prowl* [*Imbarco a Mezzanotte*]). Eventually settling in England, he directed several films, including *The Sleeping Tiger* (1954) and *The Intimate Stranger* (1956), under various pseudonyms – using for the latter film the name Joseph Walton (his first and middle names).[2] (*The Intimate Stranger* seems a displaced paradigm for the situation confronting a victim of the blacklist; its plot centers on an American film editor on the Hollywood "bad boys" list, now a successful executive producer in England, whose career is nearly ruined when an American woman unjustly accuses him of a past affair.) Ironically, with these two films, and *Time Without Pity* (1957) and *Blind Date* (1959), Losey continued to collaborate with fellow American victims of the blacklist, including Carl Foreman, Howard Koch, Ben Barzman, and Millard Lampell. But, importantly, because the prohibitions of the blacklist often extended to English films with American financial backing or dependent on American distribution (*Time Without Pity* was an exception), he had no control over his material, which was basically routine studio melodrama.

"Partly because of the typecasting nonsense in Hollywood," Losey told Milne, "after my first film I had been cast in the role of a director of melodrama. So of course when I began to work again here, I was, in the case of *The Sleeping Tiger*, handed a piece of sensational melodrama" (1968, 43). *The Sleeping Tiger* is little more than a Freudian melodrama wherein a psychiatrist studies the criminal mind by taking a delinquent (Dirk Bogarde in his first Losey film) into his home, thus creating a situation that threatens the psychiatrist's marriage to a younger American woman whose passionate nature is barely concealed beneath her gratifications in the material and class advantages of her marriage. *Time Without Pity*, which also has Freudian overtones, attacks capital punishment in a tale of a guilt-ridden, alcoholic father fighting the clock, the bottle, the authorities, and the real murderer to save his falsely accused son from execution. A more interesting film, *Blind Date*, is a skillful murder mystery with a clever twist, certainly not political except in the most extended sense. The film's most vital relationship is between the accused, a naive young Dutch artist involved with the discontented wife of an important Englishman who has powerful establishment connections, and a rude Welsh detective (Stanley Baker in his first film with Losey) who is determined to expose the truth of the crime regardless of social consequences and pressure from his own departmental superiors. *The Criminal*, whose original script Losey judged "very, very bad . . . a parody

9

of a Warner Brothers prison film" (Ciment 1985, 184), emerges from the later script by Alun Owen as both an evocative exposé of English prison life and a character study of an independent but small-time operator who dies when he competes with a formidable criminal syndicate whose power he does not comprehend.

These films, along with *The Damned* (1963), an effective polemic against the horrors of nuclear warfare, are not insignificant. Their importance, however, lies principally in what they reveal of Losey's growing sense of how to merge themes that mattered to him with the power of individualized characters set within particular social worlds, which are revealed by complex cinematic means. Losey acknowledged both his need for and frustration with the message films of this period in his artistic growth when, in speaking to Milne about *Time Without Pity*, which was adapted from a successful mystery melodrama by Emlyn Williams, he said: "We had to turn it upside down to try to make it into something with 'something to say.' I think by this time I and others in my position were somewhat hysterical in our hammering out, no matter how small the point, and probably somewhat bitter too" (1968, 44). As his work matured – and as he gained more control over his choice of material – Losey backed away from the temptations of melodrama. Even when melodramatic elements were inescapably part of a story, he sought to undercut the more obvious aspects. In *Time Without Pity*, for example, unlike the play on which it was based, the identity of the murderer is revealed at the very beginning of the film. Increasingly, Losey made his way to the center of a personal vision that outgrew (without forsaking) his simpler outrage at social or political injustice. Social themes, even "messages," had not lost their significance for him altogether, but they were subsumed by more complex attitudes and artistic forms. Thus, he remarked to Milne after the release of *Accident*: "There aren't any ready-made answers.... You can only provide a stimulation which I think at its best is some sort of complete artistic statement, which therefore is form and emotion" (42). This formulation – art as a fusion of form and emotion – is the key to understanding the development of Losey's artistic temperament and achievement.

Losey's personal artistic struggle became one of understanding the complexities and ambiguities of his characters' sexual obsessions and will to power, which are inextricably bound to their moral failings and their self-destructiveness. As he told Milne, "With *Eve* I wanted to make a picture – as I still and always do – about the particular destruction and anguish and waste of most sexual relations, whether heterosexual, homosexual, bisexual or whatever" (1968, 27). *Eve, The Servant, Accident, The Go-Between,*

The Romantic Englishwoman, La Truite, even his elegant film of Mozart's *Don Giovanni* (1979) – all testify to Losey's enduring fascination with this subject in its different cultural contexts and with its interrelated themes of class conflict, personal ambition, hypocrisy, and betrayal. What substitutes for the overt violence of the earlier melodramas is a pervasive atmosphere of anxiety, of threat, of suppressed or inner violence. Rather than a psychology of tidy answers that a film like *The Sleeping Tiger* provides, Losey came to understand what Robert Bresson stated epigrammatically in *Notes on Cinematography:* "No psychology (of the kind which discovers only what it can explain)" (1977, 39). For a director so often accused of didacticism, Losey made films after his early years that are surprisingly free of explanations and answers. Instead, what he discovered and presented most lucidly through the sophisticated narrative structures and narrational strategies of his best work is an ineluctable mystery at the heart of human nature and human behavior. Losey's films neither insist on nor ignore causality; instead his characters are more often compelled by motives that are ambiguous or uncertain rather than simple or straightforward.

Some critics have misunderstood Losey's sense of the ambiguity or mystery of characters, finding in him a cool detachment, a preference for argument rather than a concern for individual suffering and loss. "At heart a symbolist," Foster Hirsch called him, "infatuated with moral and political metaphors" (1980, 11), a teller of tales of "haunted, pursued characters ... emblematic of a larger social or political reality" (218). Losey himself would have acknowledged this tendency in his early films, but his attitudes in later films toward such characters as Hamp and Hargreaves in *King and Country* or Leo Colston in *The Go-Between* argue against such a judgment overall. Looking back on his films, Losey referred to an earlier period (*Time Without Pity, Blind Date, The Criminal*) in which "the characters were beginning to develop as real people" (Milne 1968, 46). Simple dramatic plausibility was no longer adequate; characters began to be defined by their own psychological and moral nature rather than by the social themes of the films. It is precisely the human drama that Losey had in mind when he spoke of "dealing with a subject which is harsh and cruel ... as in the case of *Accident, The Servant* or *King and Country* ... [and trying] to handle it, as I have tried to, so that people can see what beauty is there, what anguish, and have some compassion and understanding ... " (31). Indeed, anyone willing to look at Losey's films openly – that is, without preconceived dicta often as rigid as any Losey himself was ever accused of – will discover in them an insight and responsiveness to the purely human plight of his characters that is far removed from conceiving of them as mere emblems.

Like pronouncements about his supposed detachment from characters, criticism of Losey's style as visually excessive or overelaborate in a particular film is often silently extended to an evaluation of his work overall. Although frequently commented on, his style has been discussed for the most part only in a general way, and the narration in some of his best films hardly at all. The term that critics, both admiring and hostile, have most often invoked is "baroque," which Losey objected to not as inherently derogatory or inappropriate to some of his films, but as an encompassing, pseudoexplanatory label applied to his films collectively. But just what constitutes a baroque film? An apparent ornamentation, perhaps, or a self-conscious elaboration? The films of Ken Russell come to mind, as do those of other, lesser directors for whom the spectacle of their medium seems more compelling than their stories and characters. But "*Eve* was a properly baroque film," Losey believed, "because it was dealing with a baroque city, a baroque period, and essentially a baroque group of characters. It's the labelling that's troublesome" (Milne 1968, 56). By contrast, he described *The Servant, King and Country,* and *Accident* as made from scripts that "were complete in one way or another in themselves; they were entities, had their own style, from which one could develop a cinematic style" (48).

There are, of course, ongoing traces of a personal signature in Losey's films, which he believed not so much necessary as inevitable in an artist's work. In part this is a function of his unusually close and continuing relationship with the same few designers – particularly Richard MacDonald, who worked with Losey repeatedly, even on films where he was not credited as production designer. Losey's meticulous attention to visual detail was typically in the service not of verisimilitude but of stylization, "breaking down reality and reconstructing it in terms of selected things that made it possible for audiences to see only what you wanted them to see" (Ciment 1985, 167). His oft-noted fondness for mirrors in the mise-en-scène, for example, is not merely a stylistic flourish or affectation, as both *The Servant* and *The Romantic Englishwoman* make clear. In both of these films mirrors hang in houses whose decor intimately expresses the narcissism, the preoccupation with self and identity that consumes their inhabitants. "I think places are actors," Losey once said. "Houses in *Secret Ceremony* [1968], *Accident, The Servant,* these are characters for me, and they influence immensely the actions of the people who are put there" (Milne 1968, 268, 270). The same can be said of the fierce landscape in *Figures in a Landscape* (1970) against which the characters play out a drama of hostility that yields to dependence, or the images of a subdued and oppressive Paris in *Mr. Klein* in which elegant apartments and country houses seem deprived of color and richness as the Nazi roundup of Jews in World War II overtakes the central character.

If there are Losey films whose stylistic intensity is sometimes overdrawn, they are the first of his English films in which the choice of material was not his and in which the desire to "say something" from within the anonymity of his exile was still urgent. Rarely, it is true, does one see a Losey film without being aware of its visual style, but this can as easily be considered a strength as it can a weakness. In some cases – *Boom!* is a good example – Losey's visual brilliance nearly overcomes an otherwise failed effort. Speaking of his work before *Accident,* he confessed to Tom Milne his own estimate that "many of my films are...overloaded, overpacked, overdense. But dense in a different way from *Accident;* dense in the sense of trying to say too much directly instead of through people and behavior and...well, with less skill" (1968, 53). Perhaps so far as style is concerned, *Accident* is the watershed film, for its style is supremely restrained, almost severe. So, too, is style in *The Go-Between,* and yet both of these films are also unusually rich in evoking the palpable presence of their physical world as a force in its own right. In both of these films it is Losey's mode of telling the story, and its relation to characterization and the subjectivizing of time, that sets them apart from the mainstream of narrative films and defines their place among his most mature work.

Losey's finest films are characterized by a layering of unresolved tensions not just between social classes, but between calm surfaces and passionate depths, between intellect and emotion, between places and the characters who live in them, between communities and those who intrude on them. Particularly in his collaboration with Pinter, Losey explored more complex forms to express these tensions, going beyond the simple storytelling that producers typically preferred. "Many of them feel," he once lamented, "there isn't any film unless, as they put it, there is a strong storyline. This is really nonsense" (Milne 1968, 120). As his ties to the norms of traditional studio filmmaking loosened, Losey was attracted to more adventurous approaches to film form. Thus, as he turned away from the plot-centered energies of melodrama and social protest, he explored more intensively another, more important tension between what is now commonly distinguished as *story* and *discourse* – that is, the tension between a film's story (its inferrable characters and events) and the way the story is told.[3] His growing interest in subjectivity and the experience of time began to influence his sense of the resources of film to tell stories in uncommon ways and led him to such complex literary experiments in point of view and narration as Nicholas Mosley's *Accident* and Thomas Wiseman's *The Romantic En-*

glishwoman, to L. P. Hartley's *The Go-Between,* a moving study of an aging man whose life has been sacrificed to memory and loss, and finally to Proust's *A la recherche,* which he and Pinter sought unsuccessfully to make as a film.[4] In all of these the possibilities of first-person narration or character-narration assume a significant place. In fact, the complex control of narration – that is, the activity of telling a story – is of major importance in Losey's collaboration with Pinter and in his single film with writer Tom Stoppard, which was based on Wiseman's novel.[5] Both *Accident* and *The Go-Between,* for example, present substantial time-past segments that narrate their central characters' memories, and the narration in *The Romantic Englishwoman* includes scenes from a screenplay one of the characters is writing, as well as others of a seduction that may only have been imagined.[6]

In *Accident* the omniscient narration of Stephen's Oxford world reveals leisurely, civilized surfaces and characters who seem far removed from the threat of violence or a profound moral crisis, but Stephen's character-narration makes clear not only the substance of such a crisis, but its subjective aftermath, its enduring place in his consciousness.[7] So, too, for Leo Colston in *The Go-Between,* for whom returning to the sites of a boyhood holiday is a journey in which time seems suspended and the past his only reality. For both Stephen and Leo inner reality prevails over "objective" reality, and subjective realism, narrated in the mode of art cinema rather than that of classical narration, is at the heart of their stories.[8] As characters, they, like Lewis Fielding in *The Romantic Englishwoman,* live with a special vividness and self-knowledge in their memories or fantasies. Indeed, it is with memory and fantasy that these films are concerned at least as much as the observable events in the quotidian worlds the characters inhabit. Moreover, the interaction of different levels and kinds of subjectivity is central to the films' artistic forms, which reveal private worlds in which power, privilege, and passion are the stuff of an inner violence and moral failure, subjective worlds in which time both imprisons and is annihilated.

Selecting a limited number of Losey's films for analysis inevitably means making hard choices and excluding a number of works that deserve close attention. Other viewers and critics might well make different choices. *The Prowler, The Criminal, Eve* (even in its multilated state), *Figures in a Landscape, Mr. Klein, Don Giovanni, La Truite,* and *Steaming,* for example, are films from throughout Losey's career that demonstrate his range of interests and his ongoing growth as an artist. But, in our judgment, Losey's finest films are the three he made with Harold Pinter. (They are also, we would argue, Pinter's finest as a screenwriter too.) And they form the core of this book. In addition we have chosen *King and Country,* Losey's eloquent antiwar film about moral choice and growth and the inequities of class privilege, and *The Romantic Englishwoman,* a darkly witty tale of contemporary marriage, which is one of Losey's four or five films to concern itself centrally with a woman's role and experience. We have elected to begin with *King and Country,* although it was made the year after *The Servant,* principally because this order allows us to treat the progression of the Losey–Pinter collaboration in consecutive chapters while doing little violence to the chronology.

The analyses of the films will address Losey's formal experimentation with narration as it relates to characterization, subjectivity, and time. The effect of the past on the present is significant in many of his films, but the matter of time is particularly at issue in *Accident, The Go-Between,* and *The Romantic Englishwoman,* where character-narration foregrounds temporality as both a theme and a principle of the formal complexities of those films. Losey's style, his supposed distance or emotional detachment from characters, his evocative use of settings as a function of characterization, and his recurring themes will also receive close attention. Unrelenting in exposing hypocrisy and corruption, Losey increasingly focused his attention on the ways in which characters use and abuse the power inherent in personal (sexual) relations, as well as in institutions, racist societies, and social classes, and he was especially sensitive to those who were abused. If, through his work, Losey concentrated on moral failure, he did so with an understanding and compassion for human frailty and fallibility. One may ascribe his obsession with moral responsibility to his Midwest Puritan upbringing, or to his sociopolitical and artistic temperament, which was shaped by the Depression and the war years, or to his experiences during the blacklist era, when extremes of human behavior, acts of moral courage and integrity, and acts of betrayal existed side by side. What is certain, in any case, is that Losey made powerful and challenging films of both moral import and great formal beauty.

2

"What Beauty Is There, What Anguish"

King and Country

The origin of *King and Country* was an actual incident in World War I involving a young enlisted man who was executed for desertion. To this material Losey brings a keen social conscience and continuing commitment to expose hypocrisy and injustice, particularly when they are institutionalized. He also reveals a humane understanding of the personal dilemmas (emotional as well as moral and intellectual) of characters suddenly faced with circumstances in which only the most painful choices are possible. To be sure, as in such "message" films as *The Lawless, The Criminal,* and *Time Without Pity* before it, elements of melodrama are evident in *King and Country.* They are subsumed, however, by Losey's fusion of moral issues and particularized characterizations; abstractions of honor and duty are pitted against the reality of human aspirations, perceptions, and failures. Losey remarked to Tom Milne, "I set out to make a picture which, while set in World War I in a very specific and classically limited way, was to my thinking *not* a war picture" (1968, 124). As he told Ciment, "The picture is the personal relationship between that officer and that poor private deserter. . . . So that when that pistol, that *coup de grace,* has to be fired at the end, in a sense Hargreaves [the officer] is ending his own life as well as the boy's" (1985, 245). Losey's conception of *King and Country* as a personal drama going beyond an argument or protest is especially significant when one considers the appalling background against which the film is set.

In his book *Britain and the Great War, 1914–1918,* J. M. Bourne notes that the British working class was the least militarized in all of Europe when Lord Kitchener called for volunteers in August of 1914. But men like Hamp, the working-class cobbler and central figure in *King and Country,* responded, and before Christmas of that year more than a million Englishmen had volunteered. These patriotic but virtually untrained soldiers wished to win the war quickly and just as quickly get out of the army. With an unprofessional army of volunteers, the high command was convinced that the death penalty for some offenses was necessary to keep morale high. Bourne offers the following commentary: "How good was the army's morale? The final answer must be 'good enough.' There is abundant evidence of the problems. There were 25,000 courts-martial for absence without leave, 20,000 for disobedience and insubordination and 4,000 for self-inflicted wounds. Drunkenness was rife. More than 3,000 men were sentenced to death, mostly for cowardice, desertion in the face of the enemy or sleeping on duty...: 346 were actually executed" (1989, 223).[1] These figures are the more astounding when one considers that only one American soldier since the Civil War, Private Eddie Slovik in World War II, has been executed for desertion. (His story became the subject of a film, *The Execution of Private Slovik* [1974], starring Martin Sheen.) Britain, in fact, lost approximately 750,000 men in World War I. In view of such staggering carnage, the fate of a single soldier, whether just or unjust, could easily disappear, which is why Losey tells just such a story.

The man who wrote the story, Losey explained to Michel Ciment, "was not a writer; he was a defence lawyer in the court-martial. It troubled him all his life that he wasn't able to get the boy off" (1985, 244). This material was brought to Losey in the form of a radio play, whose script he thought "no more than a kind of remembered transcript of the trial" (244). But as he told Ciment, "I liked the material.... I went back to the original case. In this script, Dirk [Bogarde] figures as a writer too because he wrote some of the scenes. Since he had been an officer in the British Army, and since his family had been very much involved in the 1914–18 War, he was able to give me background and it was immensely helpful" (242). In addition to his contributions to the screenplay, Bogarde gave under Losey's direction a superb performance, one of the finest of his career, as the arrogant, self-satisfied British officer whose life is profoundly changed because, in Losey's words, he is "educated by the boy's simplicity." This comment about the character of the British officer is noteworthy because it bears on one of the most important aspects of Losey's artistic growth – his ability to integrate his impassioned attacks on social injustices with his increasingly sophisticated and subtle studies of complex characters in moral crisis.

17

In *King and Country* Private Arthur Hamp (Tom Courtenay) is court-martialed for desertion. The year is 1917. The place is Passchendaele, in the Flanders region of the Western Front. The bare facts of the case – Hamp walked away from the guns when he could stand them no more – are not at issue. The only possible defense is the youth's mental condition at the time of his act – not so much a defense, in fact, as a patchwork of mitigating circumstances: Hamp is only twenty-three years old; he volunteered for military service rather than being conscripted; he has been under fire for virtually all the three years since the war began; he is the lone survivor of the original troop with which he was sent to France; and he has recently learned in a letter from home that his wife has taken up with someone else. A pathetic list it is, unlikely to move a military court to anything except pity. Despite an eloquent plea by the officer assigned to defend him, Captain Hargreaves (Dirk Bogarde), Hamp is found guilty and sentenced to death. The field court, legally entitled to confirm its guilty verdict and temper it with mercy, declines to do so, passing the final decision to headquarters. The higher command orders Hamp's execution in the interest of "morale": the battalion is about to move into battle again. At dawn the next morning, the firing squad's volley fails to kill Hamp. Captain Hargreaves takes a pistol, walks over to Hamp, kneels and holds him while he speaks to him briefly, and then shoots him in the head, putting an end to Hamp's agony.

Without any combat scenes, *King and Country* tells a terrible story of war's injustice. More particularly, it exposes the fateful arrogance of a class-conscious officer corps all too confident of its prerogatives, and the grotesque notion that an execution for alleged cowardice, even when the allegation is demonstrably unjust, constitutes a fine and bracing tonic for young men about to face the renewed terror of trench warfare. These are strong themes, and Losey intends they should arouse moral outrage – not just in a backward glance at the Great War as history, but in a present confrontation with the film. But do such didactic intentions commandeer the film, leaving its characters stranded as mere emblems, "moral and political metaphors," as some critics would have it? Are Hargreaves and Hamp and the others denied a full measure of the fictive life that film narrative can bestow because Losey remains detached from them? Are the characters, in other words, merely agents of an argument? Certainly Losey's strong views about war's moral and political chaos, and his perhaps even stronger condemnation of hypocrisy, are crucial matters in the film. Captain Hargreaves's summation in the court-martial sequence, for example, as well as the arguments he makes in the later scene with the colonel (Peter Copley) just after Hamp has learned of his death sentence, bristle with an impolitic indignation at justice betrayed in favor of a conception of military law that reduces it to a hollow form or, in more extreme terms, that may be little more than a hypocritical ritual serving the values of a ruling class struggling to preserve its own dubious status. These themes are not unique to the Great War, of course, nor to Losey's film about it. Neither are they simply abstractions or intellectual propositions, the stuff of argument rather than feeling. For Losey does not offer characters who are mere hostages to ideas and arguments. Exactly the opposite is true: themes, issues, arguments, all compel a viewer's attention not just because of their intrinsic power, but precisely because the fate of Hamp and Hargreaves is at stake.

To discuss *King and Country* as a kind of tract, an argument whose passions belong only to the intellect, or as an allegory, whose characters exist as surrogates for contending views, is, quite simply, to deny the human drama at its heart. Doubtless the film claims viewers' attention in different ways and for different reasons, its intellectual and political views prominent among them, but no way or reason is more important, or more moving, than the complex relationship that develops between Hamp and Hargreaves. These two men, apart from elementary military formality, barely have a means of communicating at the outset, but in the end they are bound to each other by something beyond the power of even death to dissolve. They have not suddenly become friends, nor could they. Both men would find the idea ludicrous. By any social measure they have no more in common at the conclusion than when they first spoke. Each man is, from first to last, a citizen of the world he came from, a world the other can hardly grasp despite their having shared the same terrain. Their relationship changes, however, in ways that are implicitly acknowledged in the final awful moment when Hamp cannot die except Hargreaves deliver him. They have a bond, even if neither man, not even Hargreaves with his self-conscious gift for the power of words, could so much as begin to articulate it. Telling the story of that bond, its nature and its implications, is the task of the overall narration and of the various interacting stories told by the characters themselves.

King and Country shares many of its themes, in various inflections, with other films about war – among the best of them, *Paths of Glory, All Quiet on the Western Front* (both versions), *Breaker Morant, The Rack, How Many Miles to Babylon?* Not surprisingly, such films often have a measure of overt didacticism, and when there is courtroom drama, as there is in several of the films cited here, that mode's affinity for dramatizing argument makes didacticism even likelier. For all their common ground and shared intentions, however, such films can differ substantially, making comparisons between them problematic. But this is not the case with a comparison of *King and Country* to Stanley Kubrick's celebrated and brilliant *Paths of Glory*. Both Losey and Kubrick have been accused of a certain coldness, of being artists whose intellectual commitments and obsessions with style leave little room for a genuine interest in characters and still less for compassion for them. Moreover, in both story and themes *King and Country* and *Paths of Glory* share a number of important elements: common soldiers in World War I are court-martialed unjustly; officers must defend the soldiers before tribunals whose guilty verdicts are a foregone conclusion; the courts' decisions are tainted by political considerations; the rationale for the verdicts is that the executions will provide a salutary example for the condemned's fellow soldiers. Despite these similarities, however, there are differences in the two films that are significant and suggestive.

Paths of Glory exposes the moral corruption of the French high command in ordering a criminally foolish attack on an impregnable German position called the Ant Hill. When the attack fails, a terrible order is given: three men are to be chosen arbitrarily and tried for cowardice, the "explanation" for the attack's failure. The film's condemnation of military politics, personal vanity, and the callousness of great power is forceful, and the fate of the three men chosen for court-martial and certain execution is shocking. But it seems in some ghastly way only inevitable. Although the rendering of their deaths is extended and powerful, the ritualized barbarism of the execution more than the humanity of the victims is what the narration concentrates on and what horrifies the viewer. The film is most effective in dealing with the two generals, Mireau (George Macready) and Broulard (Adolphe Menjou), and their perverse minuet of elegant manners and deadly ambition. Indeed the predictability of the outcome concentrates attention on the sheer ornamentation of the generals' moves. The story of the generals' easy victory over the defense counsel, Colonel Dax (Kirk Douglas), and his humanism is what Kubrick most forcefully tells.

King and Country does not deny the existence of such characters as hold the stage in Kubrick's film. There are villains in Losey's film too, and fools and knaves enough to go around. But the victims, two very different victims, are what most concerns *King and Country*. One of the more significant differences between the two films is that *King and Country* not only admits the possibility of moral change, but concerns itself centrally with the story of such a change. That is what defines the character and experience of Captain Hargreaves. Certainly Hargreaves is not a better man than Kubrick's Dax. In fact the arrogance, the cold, almost sanctimonious rectitude ("We're all on trial for our lives") that mark him at the beginning of the film make him a good deal less likeable at first than Dax is throughout *Paths of Glory*. But considered as characters, Hargreaves is more complex than Dax, and that makes a world of difference. Hargreaves can and docs change, whereas Dax is confined by the very design of Kubrick's fiction, which excludes the possibility of change. Thus, at the end of the film Dax returns to his duty. He has spoken for humane values, but he cannot make any difference. There seems no difference anyone can make in Kubrick's film. *Paths of Glory* exposes a world in which humane values may still exist but are impotent in the face of the endless resources and power of those who control society's corrupt institutions. Colonel Dax, then, is an admirable man who is powerless so long as there is a General Broulard in the world, and Broulard and his kind are not only in the world but very much in command of it.

In *King and Country* Hargreaves, too, proves unable to change the course of the public world he lives in. But there is still a private world of conscience and choice that is not beyond reach, and that is the film's principal arena. Hamp's pitiful walk away from the guns is officially judged desertion, and he is thrust in front of a firing squad. His death, however, is not simply an example of corrupt and arrogant power, although that has dictated his fate. The army's ceremony of death in Losey's film is no less grim than in Kubrick's, but the meaning is totally different. In the shocking stillness that follows the executioners' failure, all of *King and Country*'s arguments, its sense of absolute outrage at such injustice, its "punitive fierceness," as Brendan Gill has called it, are subsumed in a moment that is absolutely private. Hamp and Hargreaves exchange their final words, and Hargreaves fires the single bullet that ends Hamp's life and changes his own forever.

Losey's film, for all its anger and despair, is finally about a mystery of human experience and about changes that are felt far more than they can be explained. Perhaps Kubrick in *Paths of Glory* believes in something better than the humankind he sees and tells his story about; that may even be his reason for telling it. But, if so, his terms seem almost philosophical rather than personal or individual, intellectual rather than emotional. Losey, on the other hand, tells a story in which loss and sacrifice are a measure of what is best in men, however dark and ironic the context, and this is what possesses one long after the arguments themselves have been forgotten.

Losey once said that "when I made *King and Country,* I thought that for once I'd made an absolutely simple classical picture, according to all the classical rules, and nobody is going to be able to say it's baroque. But they did, you know" (Gow 1971, 41). Whether he was referring to the norms of classical film narration or to the classical unities of time, place, and action is unclear. Probably both. So far as narration is concerned, the classical style with its privileging of continuity editing to emphasize spatiotemporal verisimilitude is the dominant mode. The classical unities are also generally adhered to, nowhere more obviously than in the single setting that makes for an austere, even claustrophobic film. Despite the classical simplicity that dominates (especially in the long scenes between Hamp and Hargreaves and during the court-martial), narration in *King and Country* is also highly stylized at times. The considerable complexities of the prologue and the flash cuts that appear several times during the discourse make this evident. (Also, the original release prints were entirely sepia tinted "to recall," as Losey said, "old photographs from that period" [Ciment 1985, 248]. Many of the prints now in circulation, however, are black and white.)

The crucial fact is that the film's style is the expression of a narrational, even authorial, perspective, not merely an embellishment or an end in itself, and the potential relationships of author, narrator, and character are sometimes ambiguous. Before one flash cut, for instance, Hamp tells Hargreaves that he has a son, and there follows a brief image of a child with the costumes and artificial backgrounds typical of formal photographs of the day. Similarly, when Hamp admits that his wife has taken up with someone else, two brief images follow, the first of a man lying in bed holding a cup of coffee or tea, the second a closer shot of the same thing. Are these images of Hamp's son and of his wife's new lover? Or are they figurative, not the actual people in Hamp's life but suggestive of them? Are the three images meant to be understood as originating in Hamp's consciousness, his memories or fantasies, or do they belong exclusively to the overall narration? These questions cannot be answered conclusively. The same is true of a number of other flash images – including one of the German kaiser and the king of England riding together and others presumably of the streets of Islington, Hamp's home – that appear in the same fashion. Most of the flash cuts are stills, photographs whose associations with Hamp, with history, with the overall narration of the film remain ambiguous. To whom should these images be attributed? Perhaps they are Hamp's; they could be.[2] But another possibility seems equally likely: the perspectives of the author and narrator, closely aligned in the film and present from the first frame, continue to be discernible. In other words, the omniscient narration is not neutral, nor does it pretend to be. The perspective first established in the prologue continues to make itself felt throughout the film's narration.

The style, tone, atmosphere, prevailing iconography, and even the likely resolution of *King and Country* are all evident in the richly anticipatory prologue, some of whose images are repeated later. In the juxtaposition of both its wide range of cinematic techniques and the substance of its images, this extended opening segment signals the irony that suffuses the discourse overall. Significantly, Losey's understanding of the darkness of his story and the fervor of his moral sensibility are the more powerful for his choosing irony rather than the blunter instruments of melodramatic denunciation. The mood, in fact, is reminiscent of the poignance and passion of the war poems of such youthful writers of the time as Wilfred Owen and Siegfried Sassoon, who evoked with great power the awful gulf between the heroic aspirations of young men going off to war, and the reality of desolation and death that overtook them in muddy trenches beneath the endless screaming barrages of artillery fire. The Western Front was a world in dissolution where men and animals alike decomposed and disappeared in the muddy landscape, and this is shockingly conveyed in the prologue's images of enormous explosions momentarily frozen only to dissolve in an instant into ravaged landscapes and then again into dead horses and the skeletons of soldiers half-buried in mud.

The prologue consists of two sections, and in this nearly five-minute opening, Losey uses dissolves, still photographs, freeze frames, jump cuts, rack focus, tracking camera, and a complex sound track that mixes music, background sound, silence, and voice-over. The opening shot is a low-angle long shot of a large sculpture that stands framed against the sky atop the Wellington Arch at Hyde Park Corner. Known as a quadriga, the sculpture features a bronze figure of Peace descending into a war chariot whose driver pulls up his rearing horses. By a reverse zoom, this image of peace is then juxtaposed within the same shot to the Royal Artillery Monument and a close-up view of the bronze boots of another sculpted figure, a dead World War I soldier (Figures 1 and 2). (The close-up of the foot soldier will later contribute to the closure of the film whose final shots include the muddy boots of the executed Hamp.) The tracking of the initial close shot reveals the engraved commemorative words ROYAL FELLOWSHIP beneath the dead figure. The tracking camera then reveals the end phrase: OF DEATH. The delayed disclosure of the second phrase converts the honorific into the ironic. The harmonica solo that has accompanied these images now stops. In silence the camera continues its close-up scanning of the monument's frieze depicting living and dead soldiers sprawled across a battlefield. Although the

Figure 1. The opening image of *King and Country*, the "quadriga" sculpture atop the Wellington Arch at Hyde Park, depicts the figure of Peace descending to halt a warring charioteer. (Courtesy BHE British Home Entertainment)

fluidity of the tracking shot conveys a continuity, the close-up takes in only small units at a time. The effect is a somewhat disorienting presentation of a large monument whose frieze, never seen in its entirety, appears chaotic and fragmentary. Over the sculpted war scenes is now heard the rising sound of the indifferent London traffic around Hyde Park. The long tracking shot comes to rest in a low-angle shot of the monument's sculpted howitzer, one of the few images depicting more than a partial view of any object. Suddenly, a jump cut to an artillery explosion fills the screen, sound and image shattering the momentary stasis. The tensions between sound and silence, between camera movement and static, inanimate images, between abstract compositions and recognizable forms, all resonate with the explicit war imagery embedded in the last part of the long opening shot.

A jump cut from the explosion to a medium tracking shot (almost a continuation of the opening camera movement) of the ever-present rain and mud of the trenches marks an abrupt transition to the second part of the prologue. Boots, helmets, shovels, and barbed wire are embedded in mud

Figure 2. With a reverse zoom the opening shot continues, now showing a bronze sculpture of a World War I soldier, part of the Royal Artillery Monument, which makes an ironic contrast to the allegorical figure of Peace. (Courtesy BHE British Home Entertainment)

Figure 3. The prologue concludes when this image, from a famous photograph showing the aftermath of the battle of the Somme, dissolves into the reclining figure of Hamp in his cell. (Courtesy BHE British Home Entertainment)

beside the duckboards or wooden walkway. The sound of rain and the return of the solo harmonica accompany the image that dissolves into still more mud, rain, and barbed wire until the shot rests on a broken wheel, an iconic image (which reappears as one of the last of the film) readily suggesting the cyclical, fateful, and fragmented world of the soldiers. A second artillery explosion is then freeze-framed, sudden violence becoming with equal suddenness both static and silent. This dissolves to an image of muddy shell holes that is in fact part of a larger photograph from the archives of the Imperial War Museum. The camera draws back to disclose in this same photograph a dead horse still in harness, which will return as the film's last image. The final series of dissolves of archival stills showing desolate and ravaged landscapes scarred by blasted trees ends with a close-up of the skeleton and skull of a dead soldier (a renowned photograph taken in the aftermath of the battle of the Somme; Figure 3). In voice-over, Tom Courtenay recites A. E. Housman's lines:

> Here dead lie we because we did not choose
> To live and shame the land from which we sprung.
> Life, after all, is nothing much to lose;
> Though young men think it is, and we were young.[3]

A final dissolve of this skull over a close-up of Hamp, lying on a cot and playing a harmonica, concludes the prologue.

Like an envoi closing this poetic, evocative prologue, Housman's words cast a fatalistic tone over the entire film. Courtenay's recitation (he speaks as a kind of "everyman" here, rather than in the character of Hamp) and the dissolve of the skull into Hamp's features clearly presage this soldier's fate. Even before the story begins and the characters are introduced, then, the emotive power of the film is at work, and irony has taken its place as an informing trait of the narration.

The first scene following the prologue is highly ritualized in its narration of dialogue and action as the discourse continues to delay introducing the main story events. In a kind of choric interlude, a group of soldiers who will later play a part in the story is cleaning out a large muddy shell hole or cesspit with long-handled shovels. Working in unison, the soldiers speak in fragments, completing each other's phrases. They obviously look on this task as a ritual of sorts, and their vernacular language is spoken in chantlike rhythms. The mood and attitude of men too long in the trenches are succinctly conveyed, but this scene reveals a good deal more about the film's conflicting views of human nature. (The ellipses in the following quotation indicate a change of speaker as the conversation passes from soldier to soldier.)

> Ha Ha Ha … What's this remind you of? [soldier lifts a shovelful of muck] … remind you of anything? You know, when this war is over, I think I'll get me a job in the sewer … and so you should, too … well, it's the same smell, the same company … the perfect soldier … aye, the perfect soldier … loved his country … killed rats … killed lice … went without food … without drink … without sleep … without [a soldier holds his shovel erect between his legs] … went over the top … killed the kaiser, won the war … home again … honorable discharge … fat pension … from his grateful country … women waiting for him … children fond of him … liquor is free for him … he sleeps in the sun … Remind you of anything? [soldier again lifts up the muck].

In the soldiers' words and self-mocking tone, the scatological and the heroic are combined, offering a dualistic view of man as animal (wedded to the needs and demands of his body) and man as a self-conscious entity capable of having ideals and acting heroically. His capacity to kill is, interestingly, a feature of both his creatureliness and his idealism – a theme, in various forms, in much of Losey's work.

The themes of death and dissolution already announced by the prologue are extended in this dialogue. The soldiers' talk while shoveling muck also invokes in its oblique mixture of the mundane and the profound a psychological and mythicoreligious conception of human nature of the sort that is brilliantly examined in Ernest Becker's *The Denial of Death*. Becker writes that "the anus and its incomprehensible, repulsive product represents not only physical determinism and boundness, but the fate as well of all that is physical: decay and death" (1973, 31). Becker's insight is, of course, implicit in the scene rather than explicit in the dialogue, but the inescapable irony he has grasped is persistent in the film's conception of humankind as struggling to reconcile its limits with its hopes for something nobler. Becker emphasizes man's "abject finitude, his physicalness, the unlikely unreality of his hopes and dreams" (33), but hopes and dreams are no less a necessary part of human experience than the demands of the body. If Losey's characters almost never escape their limits, neither are they entirely defined by them. Certainly Hamp and Hargreaves do not escape, but the young soldier in his simple integrity and the officer in his awkward and unanticipated moral growth define human possibilities that exceed, however ironically, the forces both physical and social that bind them.

The scene of the soldiers shoveling muck also implies the larger embedded story of "the perfect soldier," against which Hamp's career as an enlisted man and alleged deserter is unconsciously judged by those who would insist on the necessity of military (and social) forms regardless of human limits, perhaps even because of them. The perfect soldier follows the mythological path of the hero (separation, initiation, and return) by leaving home, by undergoing deprivation and suffering and doing heroic deeds, and finally by coming home with his special experience and knowledge to a hero's welcome. Joseph Campbell suggests that the hero's adventure can even begin with a mistake: "A blunder – apparently the merest chance – reveals an unsuspected world, and the individual is drawn into a relationship with forces that are not rightly understood" (1968, 51). Hamp's impulsive response to the call of king and country ("Well, when I volunteered, we didn't know any better, did we?") and to the urge to take the dare and surprise his wife and her mother by enlisting come close to a blundering into the unknown, into the human carnage that he can only describe to Hargreaves as "worse than anything."

In the ancient tradition, the separation, initiation, and return of the hero signify that he enters the world of the dead, suffers, undergoes a symbolic death and rebirth, and comes home alive and ready to share the gift of his knowledge with the living. In *King and Country,* however, the ritual pattern is invoked only to be subverted and aborted. The bewildered Hamp, separated from Islington and his bootmaker's shop, the workplace of his father and grandfather before him, found himself fighting next to a boy from up his street, a boy who was then blown to bits. "Willy's nowhere, except over me," Hamp says in his plain language to Hargreaves. "I had to get me a new uniform." Significantly, Hamp has also seen a man drown in a shell hole, and two days later Hamp himself was blown into another shell hole and nearly drowned. As he tells Hargreaves: "After that I couldn't stand it anymore.... It was like being dead, sir." Shortly after this symbolic death Hamp started walking away from the guns. When Hargreaves asks if he knew where he was walking, Hamp replies: "No. No. After I got a few miles away from the guns, I got it into my head that I was making for home ... Islington, you know. It didn't make any sense, but that's what I got into me head." Almost by accident or instinct, then, Hamp follows the hero's pattern of initiation, which proves a profoundly ironic pattern in Losey's film. Hamp's return home was an aborted one, of course, for he was arrested for desertion. As to his special knowledge, he knows only that "I reckon I'll get a fair trial.... It'll come out all right," and as he tells Hargreaves more than once, "There's nobody left in A Company that's been out here as long as me, so you see they can't shoot me."

When the court-martial convenes and the colonel begins the proceedings by reading the charge to Hamp, the language of the accusation is formal, but the meaning blunt. The penalty if Hamp is convicted is extreme, a "shooting job," Hamp remembers one of his captors saying. Hearing the charge now in the court's impersonal language, Hamp seems almost to falter, but he enters his plea of not guilty. The formalities conclude when Captain Hargreaves addresses the court, saying, "I've spoken to Captain Midgley, and we've agreed that I won't dispute the facts of the case." Hargreaves's demurrer to the facts, however, proves to be the basis for disputing virtually everything that is proffered as fact, not just within the confines of the court-martial, but within the narrative overall. In other words, although Captain Hargreaves "will not dispute the facts," the facts prove anything but agreed upon. Even their very nature, what constitutes a fact, is implicitly disputed. And not all the facts, it turns out, are created equal. Moreover, Hargreaves's position also points to one of the most significant traits of the film's narration. Story and discourse will include and depend on numerous other stories, other discourses. In an important sense, truth and justice, and historical memory, are, like Hamp's fate and Hargreaves's too, indivisible from stories. In their different roles and circumstances, many of the characters are cast as narrators. They tell stories; they raise issues, whether acknowledged by the text or not, of authority, subjectivity, reliability, interpretation, levels of narration, and their relationships.[4]

Because of Hargreaves's stipulation of the facts, the defense turns entirely on interpretation: not whether Hamp walked, but whether his walk constitutes desertion. Hamp himself never exactly opposes the official charge. Instead, his statements are mainly limited to answering the questions Hargreaves puts to him. As a result, Hamp's answers, first in his interview with Hargreaves and later in his testimony, add up not to his own best defense before a court-martial, but simply to his best effort to tell what he knows. Hamp's innate integrity makes it impossible for him to make up excuses, manufacture emotions he doesn't have, or even follow a line of questioning that might help to exonerate him. He has numerous opportunities to assert that he didn't know what he was doing, or to insist, as he once mentions, that the devil was dragging him down to his death in a watery shell hole, or that he intended to return to the battalion after his "walk." When Hamp is questioned by the colonel, Hargreaves, and Captain Midgley (James Vil liers) during the court-martial, his self-incriminating testimony simultaneously affirms his good character. Only when he tries to speak as Hargreaves would have him do, does Hamp momentarily veer from the truth. Consider the following exchange at the court-martial:

COLONEL: Private Hamp, you say you wanted to be left alone for a bit. Does that mean you intended to return to batallion?
HAMP: I don't know, sir.
HARGREAVES: That's because you don't remember anything very clearly, isn't it?
HAMP: That's right, sir... yeah.
HARGREAVES: You had no clear plan or reason in your mind, did you?
HAMP: Well, I just started going, sir. I couldn't help me-self. Well, like you told me to say, sir, I was acting under extraordinary strain... I can't... I can't think of anything else, sir.

Hamp not only reveals being coached, but he also reacts (screwing up his face) to his own false, unnatural way of speaking in Hargreaves's elevated diction ("extraordinary strain"). Hamp is simply incapable of dissembling, and out of desperation he says to Hargreaves in the presence of the court: "I'd sooner you told them, sir. You know more about it than me."

The conceptual and intentional gulf between the court's charge and prosecution, on the one hand, and Hamp's knowledge or understanding, on the other, is not only wide but crucial. Within that gulf Hamp's story is at issue in each instance of testimony and in every conversation about the case — between Lieutenant Webb (Barry Foster) and Hargreaves at the beginning, between Hargreaves and Midgley and the legal officer immediately after the case goes to the court for a judgment, and between Hargreaves and the colonel when the death sentence is confirmed. But first and most of all in the initial interview between Hamp and Hargreaves.

Having been assigned to defend Hamp, Hargreaves initially pronounces the court-martial a futile enterprise. He tells Webb that the accused (even before he has met him) is "a failure as a man and a soldier." Comparing Hamp to a dog with a broken back, Hargreaves says that one doesn't sit around talking; one shoots the dog. (Hearing Hargreaves express these views, Webb good-naturedly but pointedly asks him, "What were you like as a child?" To this Hargreaves answers flatly, "The same.") A whole world is revealed in Hargreaves's remarks and a particular view of that world. Hamp's responses to the charge and to this officer's questions limn another, radically different world and view. "We didn't know what it was going to be like, did we?" Hamp says to Hargreaves. "I didn't think about it too much, but I suppose you reckon to yourself, in my kind of life, well, it can't be much worse than this, you know. Not you, sir, but my sort, and most of the lads." Hamp never suggests that he sees himself a victim of the class differences between Hargreaves's world and his own, or that there is a fundamental inequity between the two.

Contemptuous of the accused at the outset, Hargreaves changes his mind during his interview with Hamp, whose manner of storytelling, or narration, is perhaps even more persuasive than his narrative. At one level, the acts he relates do not sound like desertion: he made no effort to hide, walked on the open road, traveled on a train, tried to talk to a priest. Somewhere along the way he got it into his mind that he was "making for home," but he recognizes that was a fantasy, not really an objective. Another aspect of Hamp's narration is even more persuasive, and that is defined by his very nature. At the trial he is called stupid; the corporal guarding him tells Hargreaves that Hamp is a "strange one." (Some reviewers have considered him a simpleton, merely a dolt.) The suggestion is that Hamp is mentally deficient, but that is to misunderstand his character. Hamp is an innocent. "For goodness and inarticulateness," Brendan Gill wrote in his review, he "is a second Billy Budd." Gill's is a fine insight, for Hamp is Billy's true descendant. But there are differences too. Hamp's is not pure goodness, an absolute force in its own right that can survive the onslaught of evil even as it is evil's victim. Rather, his is an innocence helpless to defend itself and changed inevitably by the evil of war, mortally fearful of the outcome, but an innocence that remains profoundly human and intact even at the moment of his death. Hamp has seen war; he has heard the guns; he has seen men blown to bits and other men drown in mud. He has come close to dying that way himself. He is no longer simply the young bootmaker who, on a dare, volunteered for king and country. Still, Hamp has not become cynical or crafty. He remains, like Billy Budd before him, trusting, open, even loving in this least likely of places for such qualities to endure.

In the first scene between Hamp and Hargreaves, which is quite long, Losey relies principally on long takes in which the subtly shifting relationship between the accused and his defender is revealed by the mise-en-scène even more than the dialogue and action. Hargreaves dominates the beginning of the scene by virtue of his rank and the circumstances. Without being overtly challenged by Hamp, he nonetheless loses the initiative to the youth's straightforwardness. Hamp is never less than respectful, even humble, but his humility is of a piece with his honesty. For Hargreaves, unlike the officers of the court-martial who will formally judge Hamp, the youth's defense proves not to lie in the confines and definitions of military law, but in his shockingly exposed humanity. Losey reveals the greater depth of this en-

31

Figure 4. A high-angle shot marks the beginning of the interrogation scene in *King and Country* when Hargreaves first meets Hamp. (Courtesy BHE British Home Entertainment)

counter as Hargreaves's superior place in the images yields to Hamp's. Moreover, from the beginning of the scene when Hargreaves's authority seems unchallenged, the images undercut this perception, for they are crowded with the visible evidence of this war-torn moment, the tentative, dark quiet of a temporary command post and its pathetic cell in which Hamp and Hargreaves are equally vulnerable to the forces of death that have brought them face to face. As Hamp tells his story, the mise-en-scène increasingly centers on him until finally, in a single image that favors them equally, the two men, so unequal in their status, sit on the same bench talking to each other (Figures 4–6). Losey's point is not simply the subversion of Hargreaves's military authority, but a prefiguring of the conclusion in which both men will be victims.

Later, during the trial, Hargreaves addresses the members of the court: "Private Hamp is not a liar. He is not glib. He has no ready answers. He has an embarrassing honesty that made him a bad witness in his own case." So far as the court and its verdict are concerned, Hargreaves is right, although one wonders finally if anything Hamp might have said would have made him a better witness and altered the outcome. Hargreaves's charac-

Figure 5. Hamp's prominence in the image suggests the already shifting relationship between these two men who are so unequal in their military and social status. (Courtesy BHE British Home Entertainment)

Figure 6. In its progression of images, which culminates in this shot of the two men seated together, the interrogation scene prefigures the film's conclusion in which both Hamp and Hargreaves will be victims. (Courtesy BHE British Home Entertainment)

terization of Hamp, however, speaks to the qualities that do make him the most credible of witnesses. Furthermore, the process whereby Hamp's credibility is tested proves the model for testing all the narrations. That is, questions of authority, reliability, and interpretation that are raised by any narration are here made overt and tested within the discourse itself. Captain Midgley, the prosecutor, and Captain O'Sullivan (Leo McKern), the medical officer, for example, have their own individual and eccentric attitudes toward Hamp and his story, attitudes that focus attention on the officers' personal and professional authority and reliability as interpreters. Midgley effectively cross-examines all witnesses and misses no opportunity to portray Hamp in unfavorable ways as an undistinguished soldier, as a malingering coward, and even as a shrewdly calculating deserter masquerading as a simpleton. Midgley skillfully makes his case against Hamp, but without personal animus; in fact, his personal feelings contrast with his courtroom tactics. Midgley can later tell his adversary with sincerity: "You did very well, Hargreaves. I hope you got him off." As if to counter this sentiment, the legalistic Midgley adds: "But, you know, a proper court is concerned with law. It's a bit amateur to plead for justice." Still later, before the verdict is in, Midgley encourages Hargreaves to violate protocol and visit the anxious Hamp because "it would be kind." Unlike Midgley, the pompous and insensitive Captain O'Sullivan views Hamp's guilt as confirmation of his professional competence as a doctor. Where Hamp is uncertain about his state of mind when he walked away from the guns, O'Sullivan is all certainty in judging him a coward. O'Sullivan's version of things covers his own indifference, if not incompetence. According to O'Sullivan, Hamp did nothing less than "turn and run."

Although the colonel in *King and Country* is not portrayed with the ruthlessness and self-aggrandizing egomania associated with Kubrick's generals in *Paths of Glory,* he is nonetheless coldly protective of power and privilege. Such class considerations inevitably raise questions about hypocrisy. Losey himself characterized *King and Country* as "a story about hypocrisy, a story about people who are brought up to a certain way of life ... and who finally have to face the fact that they have to be rebels in society, that they have to be outlaws and outcasts and outsiders in society for the rest of their lives, with all the penalties this entails, or else they have to accept hypocrisy" (Milne 1968, 125). Hargreaves, however, is the only character for whom this seems unmistakably true.

The crisis of conscience that Losey speaks of is evident at the court-martial and its aftermath, where the colonel in effect seeks to wash his hands of the whole affair. Hargreaves frames his closing argument to the court by

34

contrasting Hamp's confused state of mind at the time of his desertion with the court's responsibility for its actions. "This court," he argues, "has the power to choose. . . . I beg to remind the court that if justice is not done to one man, then other men are dying for nothing." This constitutes the film's most overt statement of a social and moral theme in the fashion of Losey's earlier work, but for all its importance this is not the climax or the thematic center of *King and Country*. Silence and a slow pan of the faces in the room convey the impact and persuasiveness of Hargreaves's plea until the colonel dismissively replies, "Matter of opinion." The colonel remains unswayed by either the logic or emotion of Hargreaves's speech, but his position is defined more by his equivocations than by his convictions. Informed shortly after the trial that he may confirm Hamp's sentence himself or send it to a higher authority, the colonel orders others to prepare a finding and have it sent off for confirmation.

The highly structured events in *King and Country* (a court-martial, a priest's visit to a condemned man, a firing squad) reflect Losey's view of the centrality of ritual in social and moral life, and they suggest his sense that men may envelop themselves in such rituals rather than accept the burden of individual judgment and choice. In the scenes between the colonel and Hargreaves, even the smaller rituals of military etiquette can be significant. When the death sentence is confirmed by headquarters, the distraught Hargreaves goes to the colonel. Saying nothing, but nearly gagging on the scotch the colonel offers him, Hargreaves is reprimanded for his breach of decorum in sullenly gulping down the drink. To the colonel's comment, "Rather short on ceremony, aren't we?" Hargreaves responds, "Yes, I had too much of that today." Relatively insignificant in itself, this exchange reveals the officers' ceremonious world of rank and class. The exchange also suggests Hargreaves's ongoing struggle with his role in these rites, a struggle brought to a crisis through his unanticipated relationship with Hamp. Hargreaves is again cautioned for "overstepping" when he tells the colonel that Hamp's execution means they have all lost and they are all murderers. Hargreaves questions the rationale of killing Hamp to maintain morale; in response the colonel first affirms the rightness of the verdict but then admits to sharing something of Hargreaves's doubts. The colonel's admission calls everything into question, as Hargreaves's moment of recognition and stunned silence suggests. Through formalities, however, the colonel rescues the situation, dismissing Hargreaves by asking him "on your way out" to deliver a "next of kin" letter to Webb, the officer in charge of Hamp's execution. The colonel is no amateur gamesman in protecting his position. Not only has he turned Hargreaves into errand boy in the service of the execution, but he has set in motion the procedure to punish Webb (a fear that Webb has previously confided to Hargreaves). A knowing smile at the mention of Webb's name indicates Hargreaves's recognition of the predictable but skillful manipulations of his superior officer, who says of Webb's relationship to Hamp, "his man, his platoon, his mistake... teach him a lesson."

Also at issue in this scene are both men's versions of the "facts," an issue at the center of much of Losey's work because ambiguity is so often falsely clothed as certainty. Facts for Hargreaves include Hamp's "technical desertion," which was really no more than "a bloody little walk"; for the colonel, the facts are his received orders to execute Hamp in order to boost the morale of the battalion moving into combat the next day. Because of his empathy for Hamp, Hargreaves has come to a more imaginative understanding of facts, an understanding that accepts the uncertainty of human motives and the complexity of human character.[5]

In the film, the playing out of rituals, whether social (class), military, or religious, establishes a kind of mad order in the midst of chaos. Even the enlisted men, those most subject to the cruelties of this hierarchical world, get Hamp drunk and, to allay their own fears, enact an execution of the condemned man. Unlike their earlier mock trial of a rat, which Losey himself called "slightly cardboard" (Milne 1968, 126) and "the least successful thing in the film" (Ciment 1985, 246), this dark revel before the execution conveys the confused and contradictory feelings of the men – their drunkenness, their fear, their homoeroticism, their need to comfort and be comforted, and their concern for and cruelty to Hamp. Whatever the opiate, whether drink, religion, or drugs, the men use it to blot out their anxieties and anguish over the condemned man now victimized by the war and by the indifference or cruelty of men (the officers, the doctor, the padre, and the enlisted comrades themselves) pledged to help him.

The drunken antics of Hamp's comrades are interrupted by Lieutenant Webb and the padre (Vivian Matalon). In the harrowing scene that follows, the blindfolded Hamp shouts after his runaway companions and blindly grasps hold of the padre, who has come to absolve Hamp of his sins. Like the doctor, Captain O'Sullivan, the padre proves to be so removed from Hamp's needs and feelings that his ministrations are cruelly, if unintentionally, misguided. Stressing a chastening and scourging God whose great mercy forgives all sins, the padre condemns as he tries to comfort; his abasement of the already victimized and abandoned Hamp is a ghastly ritual that serves to comfort only the dutiful and self-absorbed priest. His devotion to ritual is paired with his indifference to Hamp (Figure 7). When Hamp then vomits the communion wafer and wine, Lieutenant Webb intervenes to pump a syringe full of a soporific drug into the pitiful soldier. Although the padre insists that Hamp's soul is present in the room, Webb is more honest and aware of the consequences of his action. Over the drunk and drugged Hamp, Webb declares, "All that's here is a few hours of bloody nothing."

The horror that surrounds the firing squad scene at the end of *King and Country* comes from the realization that, on the most pragmatic level and on the ritual level as well, Hamp's death seems meaningless. Hargreaves and even the colonel have expressed their doubts about how efficacious Hamp's execution will be in raising morale or instilling courage in the troops. Nor is Hamp a successful scapegoat; his death is obviously unlikely to lessen the chances of the other soldiers' dying in battle – quite the reverse seems to be the case. As Private Sparrow says while cradling and comforting the drunken Hamp just hours before his execution: "Here today, gone tomorrow. It doesn't matter who kills you, does it? Well, you've lived a long life, Hamp, and you're due. You rot in the mud and that's that. Doesn't matter what anyone bloody well thinks about it, does it? Hey, we're all moving up soon. We'll be in the same boat as you are. We'll all be rat food before long." In context, this grim, cliché-ridden, desperate consolation of Private Sparrow's also has the terror of truth about it (Figure 8). Even that which might be taken as ironic in Sparrow's speech ("you've lived a long life, Hamp, and you're due") rings true when we remember Hamp's three years in the trenches that have left him the sole survivor of his unit.

In their last full scene together, Hamp tells Hargreaves, "You've taught me a lot of things, sir, and I'm grateful." Hargreaves answers, "Have I? Rather too late, I fear." Although learning things too late is a familiar pattern in tragedy, Hamp is not a tragic figure. What Hamp has learned through his articulate defender and spokesman is not altogether clear. If Hargreaves speaks the truth for the confused Hamp, the young private learns little more than that he unthinkingly walked away from the guns, that he should have done his duty, and that he must now submit to military law. Whatever Hamp's capacity for anguish or self-knowledge, it has neither the depth nor scale of classical tragedy, or even of a Paul Baumer in *All Quiet on the Western Front*. Furthermore, in the final hours Hamp's suffering is obviated through Webb's hypodermic and the enlisted men's rum. What dignity he has in the end finds expression in his brief exchange with Hargreaves after the botched execution.

Blindfolded and tied to a chair, Hamp is carried almost senseless to the execution site. Shown from a perspective behind the firing squad, it appears

Figure 7. In contrast to the brutally honest Private Sparrow, the self-absorbed padre offers ritual prayers that only add to Hamp's terror and abasement. (Courtesy BHE British Home Entertainment)

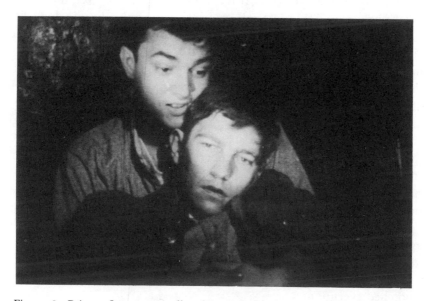

Figure 8. Private Sparrow cradles the condemned Hamp and consoles him with the grim observation, "We'll all be rat food before long." (Courtesy BHE British Home Entertainment)

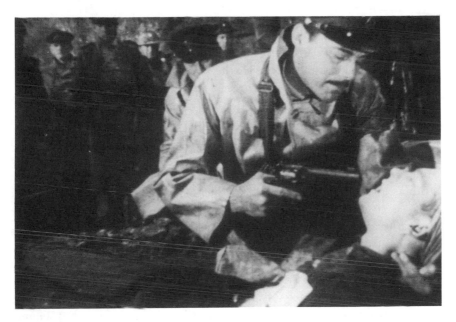

Figure 9. The final, fatal exchange between Hargreaves and Hamp. (Courtesy BHE British Home Entertainment)

that some of the men intentionally fire off target. In any case, the execution fails, and O'Sullivan, removing Hamp's blindfold, announces as much. When Webb slowly draws his pistol and then hesitates, Hargreaves takes the gun from him and walks over to Hamp. Cradling Hamp's head on his arm, Hargreaves asks, "Isn't it finished yet?" Hamp replies, "No sir, I'm sorry." In this bitterly ironic exchange both military and class distinctions between them are implicitly acknowledged, but so is their mutual concern and respect.

In addition, subtle and ironic religious connotations are invoked here. A passage from Bourne's *Britain and the Great War* provides an illuminating context within which to view this scene:

> If England's cause was just, if the war was a struggle between good and evil, then it followed that England's cause was also God's. The concepts of suffering, redemption and renewal lay at the heart of Christian faith. Their imagery came naturally to people brought up on the Bible, the Book of Common Prayer, the Protestant Hymnal and *The Pilgrim's Progress*. The Church, too, for its part, had long made use of the imagery of war. The idea of the 'Christian Soldier' assumed a new meaning and significance. Christ's example was the

war's inspiration and justification. 'Greater love hath no man than this, that a man lay down his life for his friends.' Christ's sufferings offered many parallels with that of the soldier. The war's poetry is full of them. 'He stood before me there,' Sassoon wrote of an ordinary Tommy. 'I say that He was Christ.' (1989, 230–1)

Christian faith and the influence of the church were undeniably powerful forces throughout the war. *King and Country,* however, has already called into question the ministrations of a priest blind to the needs of the condemned Hamp, and the execution scene raises the issue of Hamp's death as a spiritually redemptive sacrifice. However much one may want to see such significance in the film, Losey's deeply ironic view allows for no transcendent resolution. Bourne may rightly claim that "Christ's suffering offered many parallels with that of the soldier," but Hamp's stupefied anguish, as well as his innocence, ordinary goodness, and truthfulness, only accentuate the unfairness, the despair, the pathos of his death.

Hargreaves's question – "Isn't it finished yet?" – may recall Christ's last words on the cross – "It is finished" (John 19:30) – but Hamp, however Christ-like, can neither save nor be saved. Defined against rather than by military and religious rituals, Hamp and Hargreaves play out their fate. In any traditional sense, Hamp's death accrues little meaning as a sacrifice. His dying hardly gives life to the community, or if it does, it maintains an unjust and hypocrital society. The ritual surrounding Hamp's death does not express the sacred or point to a hoped-for spiritual transcendence. Still, something other than despair resonates with the pistol shot that ends Hamp's life (Figure 9). Horrific as that moment is, it defines Hargreaves's sacrificial act, an act confined to the human plane of existence and fraught with sorrow, guilt, and love. The anguish here is as much Hargreaves's as Hamp's. Thus, the question becomes what Hargreaves has learned from Hamp. Not duty but a sense of humanity, a personal commitment to Hamp, necessitates his action. Hargreaves is changed forever through this relationship; what he learns about his own contradictory nature and about his capacity for compassion can best be measured against the smug and arrogant Hargreaves who at the beginning prejudged Hamp a failure as a man and soldier while he glibly pronounced, "We're all on trial for our lives." In retrospect, Private Sparrow's questions to Hamp – "It doesn't matter who kills you, does it?" and "Doesn't matter what anyone bloody well thinks about it, does it?" – are not merely rhetorical. It matters to Hargreaves. In choosing to fire the pistol himself,

Hargreaves transforms a bungled public ritual into a personal sacrifice, an act of love, mercy, and expiation.

That war is a horror that undermines even the loftiest of civilizations hardly needs saying. But of course, it does need saying, over and over again. The task is ancient and more than honorable, however futile it may seem, and *King and Country* takes its place in that tradition. But Losey's film is more than an eloquent jeremiad. Folly and evil are all too apparent in its tale, but Losey is drawn to the human reality of the social and moral themes that compel his attention. He is no longer the polemicist, however skillful, if he was ever merely that. Neither is he merely a stylist. And, one must remember, the temptation to find a more suitable label is clearly one that he would have rejected. The film is better served by simply recognizing its own powerful terms: a callous determination to enforce military order (and its social forms) fatefully intersects with the life of a single, powerless young man and then unexpectedly with the life of another man whose status would have seemed proof against such a calamity. The first man dies, and the second is irrevocably changed, although his social position, his place in the army and the world he comes from, seems not in the least changed. *King and Country* indicts in the most forceful terms the false values that betrayed both men, but even more it reveals, as Losey said he hoped it did, "what beauty is there, what anguish" (Milne 1968, 31). Losey's words here, almost wistful as they are, express his deepest intentions as an artist, summing up his attitude not just toward *King and Country,* but toward all the films to be discussed in the following chapters. Needless to say, the films are not identical in themes or tone; no single note is relentlessly struck. Victims, however, are his persistent concern, whether victimization is imposed on characters by forces outside themselves or born of their own human failings.

3

"An Extension of Reality"

The Servant

"While I was in Rome, working on *Eve*," Losey told Michel Ciment, "Dirk Bogarde rang to tell me that there was in existence a Harold Pinter script from *The Servant*.... Actually, I had taken the novel *The Servant* [by Robin Maugham] to Dirk just ten years before. I got in touch with Harold whom I'd known before. It was a very uneven but absolutely brilliant script" (1985, 224).[1] Rights to the Pinter script were purchased with funding arranged by Losey's agent Robin Fox, the father of James Fox, the young actor who subsequently gave an exceptional performance as the ill-fated Tony. (At the time of his original interest, Losey apparently had Bogarde in mind for Tony rather than the servant Barrett, the role he eventually played with such insinuating power.) *The Servant* proved to be the film that changed Losey's artistic life and reputation once and for all. "So with [Richard] MacDonald and Dirk Bogarde and with my various hurts and destructions," he told Ciment, "I had a kind of rising from the ashes on *The Servant*" (179). A cool reception when the film premiered at the Venice festival was soon forgotten in the enthusiasm of its openings in New York and London and, a few months later, in Paris. Thus, at the age of fifty-four, with his fifteenth feature film, Losey had his first international success. More important, despite a contentious first meeting with Pinter, he had found his ideal collaborator as screenwriter.

The Servant is especially significant for what it reveals about Losey and Pinter's discovery of the possibilities of a common voice. So far as English society was concerned, both were outsiders, although obviously in different ways. Losey was the expatriate American struggling to come to terms with another society even as he was in exile from his own; Pinter was the bright and talented son of a working-class family with limited access to the privileges so available to the upper classes in his own country. Despite this common ground, the son of a Jewish tailor living in Hackney, in London's East End, and the American midwesterner educated in the Ivy League would seem unlikely collaborators. Commenting on their disparate backgrounds, however, Losey saw this as an advantage. "The two of us together," he told Ciment, "can have a look at aspects of England that probably no others in the world could have" (1985, 262).

Other traits, too, might seem obstacles to their successful collaboration, none more so than the gulf between the tendency toward "baroque romanticism" of Losey's visual style and Pinter's oblique, elliptical language. But their artistic differences, like the differences in their cultural backgrounds, became the basis for a new, more expressive vision for both men, one in which visual richness and understated, suggestive language did not contradict each other but were joined in a provocative tension. Noting that Pinter's scripts "superbly evoke the visual for me," Losey said that "the screenplays that Harold has done with me...are absolutely different from anything that he's done for anybody else. His screenplays always have their personal stamp, there is no doubt about that. But if you look at some of the other films he's made, they are not the same films as the films he makes with me" (Ciment 1985, 242). The screenplay for *The Servant*, however, does bear a noticeable resemblance to the playwright's stage dramas. The often elliptical dialogue and strangely disturbing tone of scenes in which the subtext seems more compelling (and somehow menacing) than anything in the text itself suggest such Pinter plays of this period as *The Birthday Party* (1957), *The Caretaker* (1959), and *The Homecoming* (1964). And this is not always to *The Servant*'s advantage. For all the film's brilliance and disturbing power, the tension between text and subtext is occasionally too insistent. Moreover, a striking shift in style and characterizations intrudes in the last third of the film. To some extent the latter arises from the original material; Maugham's novella is weakest in its last section, which attempts to resolve the narrative without fully confronting the psychological and social issues of sexuality and power it has raised. The shift in style reveals that the brilliant possibilities of the collaboration between Losey and Pinter are not yet fully realized in their first film together. In their next two, *Accident* and *The Go-Between*, however, they succeed in fusing their different strengths to achieve wonderfully subtle and expansive films. Looking back on their work, Losey summed it up by remarking: "We got to understand each other very well and to trust each other completely. And I think it's the best and most useful collaboration I've ever had" (240).

In *Hollywood U.K.*, Alexander Walker, always a perceptive critic of Losey's films, examines *The Servant* within the sociopolitical context in which it was produced: "This year, 1963, was the year of rumours, doubts, suspicions and scandals about public figures and people in high places in England whose confluence was such that, by the time the Losey film was ready, it threatened virtually to destroy all credibility in our rulers and 'our betters' " (1974, 205). The year 1963 saw the Profumo scandal, the downfall of the Macmillan government's minister of war, which was set in motion by his sexual entanglement with a young model. Making clear that he is not "suggesting any *post hoc, propter hoc* relationship," Walker goes on to say that

> within its own terms *The Servant* had managed to conceptualize a state of change in British society which . . . was forcing self-knowledge on to people who had been hidden from it by their own sedulously fostered division of life into public and private sectors with appropriate, though hypocritically unreconcilable, standards of conduct for each. *The Servant* was one of the events that breached this moral *cordon sanitaire;* it isolated something British society already felt stirring, and because it was a work of art that was all of a piece (or very nearly) it permeated one's cultural consciousness more profoundly than any British film had done since [Karel Reisz's] *Saturday Night and Sunday Morning.* (208)

The central conflict in *The Servant* exposes the arrogant, self-indulgent corruption of a privileged class dependent on exploiting an underclass whose servility is but a thin veil for long-standing resentments and desires. But the film goes beyond an indictment of social or class inequities, and beyond melodrama as well, in its shocking tale of a master and servant mutually destroyed. Both characters are too individualized and complex to be construed as broadly as ideological melodrama would require. True, politics is plainly at work here; so, too, are good and evil. But the film cannot be explained by politics alone, nor simply as a morality tale – if such tales can ever be termed simple. Rather, it tells the story of a collapse, both personal and societal, in which false values, the politics of class, the vagaries of desire, and the power of uncertain sexuality claim equal places in a world suffused with hypocrisy. In its tale of a destruction that seems both eccentric and inevitable, *The Servant* joins themes and character in a fashion that marks a significant step for Losey in his journey from the relative simplicity of social commitment to sensitivity to the dilemmas of individual characters in a complex social and moral world.

In various ways the principal characters in the film are all destroyed. Tony hires Barrett, the manservant who takes over the decorating of Tony's recently purchased Chelsea town house and who eventually brings Vera (Sarah Miles), a young woman supposedly his sister but in fact his mistress, into the house as a maid. Despite opposition from Tony's fiancée Susan (Wendy Craig), Barrett comes to control the weak and sybaritic master. Fulfilling Barrett's plan, Vera seduces Tony, who then drifts away from his already listless relationship with Susan. When Tony and Susan discover Barrett and Vera having sex in the master's bedroom, Tony, who seems shattered by the discovery, orders the pair from the house. Despite his plea that she stay with him, Susan leaves Tony also. In an emotional limbo, Tony, who is unable to care for himself, later rehires Barrett, who claims that Vera was responsible for all that happened. In the haze of drink and drugs that follows, Tony soon sinks into a world of degradation and ambiguous sexuality. The servant, now the corrupt and corrupting master of the house, eventually brings Vera back and locks Susan out one last time. With the roles now fully reversed, the servant secures the house and locks on to his victim in a symbiotic-parasitic relationship that imprisons and destroys both men.

From the beginning the house and the changes it undergoes give shape to a story of human possibilities perverted, of destruction that engulfs all those who enter it. The importance of Richard MacDonald's set design and Douglas Slocombe's cinematography can hardly be overestimated, for the spatial design and furnishings of the house and the lighting and photography of this setting are inextricably joined to the film's atmosphere and its themes. The empty house invites its inhabitants to decorate it, to fill it with both objects and actions, to make it their own. As a result, the house becomes what Losey calls "an extension of reality," a metaphor for conflicting, sometimes contradictory, desires. Lacking any self-awareness, or even a strongly defined personality, Tony implicitly extends a fatal invitation to the servant to become the dominant force. Tony, the dreamer of romantic notions about building great cities in the South American jungle (yet another environment), having only the vaguest ideas of what his own house should be, relies on Barrett, whose first task in looking after Tony is to supervise

45

the decoration and furnishing. Turning his hand to that task, the servant is soon exerting an influence on his master that foreshadows the role reversal to come.

The mise-en-scène of the first sequence – Barrett's arrival for his interview with Tony and the interview itself – establishes the pattern of fluid circular camera movements that informs the film's visual style. The few cuts in the sequence are confined to the first moments of Barrett's arrival. Once Tony shows Barrett to an upstairs room for their principal discussion, the remainder of the sequence is presented in a single, predominantly circular shot punctuated only by occasional pauses. In the opening shot the camera, tilted upward, tracks backward along a row of trees, their branches barren against a wintry sky, gradually turning until it comes to the facade of a building. The camera then pulls back for a wider angle that shows Barrett standing on a sidewalk just below the sign "Thomas Crapper, Sanitary Engineers." (Whether this juxtaposition is meant as a pun on Barrett's origins or character is arguable, but all the same, a scatological background is wryly linked to the man with his umbrella, topcoat, and hat – not a bowler, of course, for Barrett is not a gentleman but "a gentleman's gentleman.") Continuing its circle, the camera follows Barrett as he walks toward Tony's house. Finding the door unlocked, he enters the house unannounced. An interior shot pans from Barrett's entrance to a view of the staircase (a central battleground of the ensuing struggle) and holds for a time until Barrett reenters the frame, crossing to the stairs and ascending the first step or two. The shot continues to track as he moves from the entrance hall to explore adjoining rooms. Eventually, through a series of open doorways Barrett sees in the distance the sleeping figure of Tony, who has had "too many beers for lunch." Lacking any furnishings or ornaments, the house is defined thus far only in terms of empty spaces and shapes, the succession of doorways, and the figure stretched out on a deck chair. As Barrett stands over Tony, a series of alternating shots (high angles looking down on Tony and low angles looking past the reclining Tony in the foreground to Barrett) further anticipate the struggle for dominance that will define this relationship (Figure 10). Awakened by Barrett, Tony rouses himself, and for a time his boyishly easy charm and aristocratic insouciance tend to override the initial impression of a passive young man lacking energy or direction.

Once they are in the upstairs room, which is empty except for two chairs set rather incongruously in the middle of the space, Tony asks Barrett to sit. Although Tony sits briefly in the other chair, he is soon up and walking about the room. Standing over and circling around the seated Barrett, Tony seems easily to dominate the interview with his questions and comments.

But the image tells another story. The single sustained shot (two minutes, thirty seconds) combines Barrett's stationary position, Tony's wandering about, and the camera's own fluid movement to effect a constantly changing mise-en-scène in which first one character and then the other dominates the image (Figure 11). If Tony stands while Barrett sits, and his freedom of movement in the image expresses his superior social status and the advantage he has in making the decision about employing Barrett, Barrett is nonetheless often in the foreground of the frame dominating the image. The result is a visual counterpoint that calls into question the apparent social meaning of the scene. Beyond dialogue and events that are ordinary, the image establishes the potential drama of class conflict and personal domination within this seemingly undramatic encounter. At its conclusion Tony admits to needing "well, everything... general looking after... you know." A deferential Barrett, ready to assume the task, smiles and answers, "Yes, I do, sir." Like a patient spider, Barrett watches Tony move casually about the room even as the mise-en-scène signals that Tony has already begun to entangle himself.

Under Barrett's watchful eye, the house takes shape and becomes almost a physical extension of the servant himself, who winces as the workmen clumsily nick newly painted woodwork. When Tony first shows the redecorated house to Susan, he unintentionally reveals Barrett's already considerable control. Susan is amused by Tony's naive enthusiasm for his new surroundings, but she is also dismayed by his lack of concern for the way Barrett has everywhere imposed his tastes. Unaware of this, Tony proudly unveils to Susan the chic new sculpture that Barrett has installed in the garden, an abstract that metaphorically suggests Tony's own shapeless character. As if intuitively, Susan seems to realize that the servant has constructed a pleasure house that is a prison, and she reacts against Barrett and the hermetic environment he is creating.

Susan is an intrusion from the outside world, and she and Barrett will be locked in combat over Tony's life and soul. Their struggle begins with Susan's initial response to the interior decorating. The portraits of aristocrats that hang on the walls are reminders of the past, of an elegant and refined, if contradictory, world now dead, along with Tony's father and Lord Barr, Barrett's former employer, both of whom died within the same week. But as heir to this world, Tony is overrefined, almost effete, without individuality or purpose, except for his absurd rationalizing talk, his romanticized version of noblesse oblige about building a civilization for the poor of Asia Minor out of the Brazilian jungle. When Susan first enters the newly decorated living room and examines the paintings, Barrett tells her that "the simple

Figure 10. In their first meeting in *The Servant*, Tony's prominence in the image is undercut by Barrett's position standing over him. (Courtesy Weintraub Entertainment Ltd.)

Figure 11. During the job interview, Tony moves freely about the room, seemingly dominating the patient Barrett, whose servitude has already begun to entrap the unwary aristocrat. (Courtesy Weintraub Entertainment Ltd.)

Figure 12. A stylized tableau offers a satirical look at the smug and insular aristocrats, the Mountsets. (Courtesy Weintraub Entertainment Ltd.)

and classic is always best." Susan, objecting that the paintings aren't classic but "prehistoric," rejects this carefully arranged, superficially aristocratic world that will soon turn decadent. Her conflict with Barrett becomes more apparent in their quiet but intense struggle over the decor during one of Susan's visits to Tony when he is in bed with a cold. At first Barrett rather ostentatiously occupies himself with dusting books and spraying the house with disinfectant. But when he tries to remove the flowers that Susan has brought into Tony's sickroom, she insists the flowers stay. On a later occasion when Tony is not present, she tries to assert her authority over Barrett by changing the decor with colored pillows and flowers and by emphatically treating him as a servant who must light her cigarettes and follow her orders.

Susan is herself a problematic character who, even when successfully deflating Tony's pretensions, seems nonetheless a snob in her attacks on Barrett. Although one may sympathize with her struggle against the insidious servant, her eagerness to demean him may well expose her own cruel assertion of class privilege. There is in fact a general uncertainty about Susan's values, attitudes, and motivations.[2] Interestingly, her role in the film is greatly expanded from that of the sweet girlfriend, Sally, in Maugham's novella. Sally waited for Tony during his tour in the army and hoped to

49

marry him. Although she dislikes Barrett intensely and opposes him in her modest way, Sally has no ongoing confrontations with him. Angered by Tony's obsession with the many comforts that Barrett provides and frustrated by Tony's inattention to her, Sally gives up on him reluctantly and sadly when she marries another man and moves to a farm in Rhodesia. On the other hand, Susan, who also eventually says she loves Tony, disappears and then reappears in the film only to be finally excluded by Barrett. Although she wins some battles, Susan is ultimately humiliated by the servant as she attempts and fails to save Tony.

Barrett, who can anticipate and even create Tony's desires, controls the feckless aristocrat by making him a prisoner of his own senses. Once Barrett introduces Vera to the scene, he is in nearly total control. A provocative but enigmatic tool in the servant's schemes, Vera seduces Tony, who becomes sexually obsessed with her and thus steadily more bound to the house. When maid seduces master (appropriately, in the kitchen) the heightened use of sound – water dripping from a tap, the ticking of a clock, the loud ringing of an unanswered telephone (presumably a promised evening call from Susan) – creates a charged atmosphere that combines with Vera's sensual teasing pose on the kitchen table to entice and entrap Tony. The centripetal pull of the house and its sensual pleasures grows ever stronger on Tony. Even dreary weather, rain and snow, contributes to the oppressive atmosphere that draws him back to the house and to the solicitous services of both Barrett and Vera.

Shortly after the seduction scene, Pinter's simultaneously mundane and suggestive dialogue, modulated with telling (and typical) silences and pauses, draws on the weather motif when Barrett, showing Susan to the door, finds an offhand and indirect way of suggesting that he has the upper hand in their competition for Tony. He says to Susan, "I'm afraid it's not very encouraging, miss . . . the weather forecast." In a similar vein, on an earlier occasion Barrett arranged a weekend away from the house, leaving Tony and Vera alone. When he returns and correctly surmises that Tony and Vera have slept together for the first time, the two men have the following banal exchange about Vera that the servant nonetheless invests with considerable innuendo:

BARRETT: I notice she didn't do the washing up.
TONY: Still under the weather, I suppose.
BARRETT: Under the what, sir?
TONY: The weather.
BARRETT: Oh yes.

The subtext of much of the dialogue in such scenes is matched by the complexity of the images. A familiar signature of Losey's style in many of his films is the elaborate use of mirrors. Perhaps first evident in *The Servant,* they are an integral part of the decor, of the "tasteful and pleasant surroundings" that Barrett is so anxious to create. When the image focuses directly on a single character, a doubling effect frequently occurs because the character is reflected in a mirror. Such doubling (sometimes even tripling) suggests the divided personalities of the central characters, as well as their self-indulgent, narcissistic attitudes and contests. In fact, the first view of the completely decorated interiors of the house is presented as a reflection in a convex mirror. The image of the living room in which the mirror hangs is clear, but the mirror warps its appearance. Also, the multiple mirrors often reflect the triangular arrangement of the characters as their complex emotional and psychological relationships shift (Figure 13).

One scene making skillful use of such mirroring involves all four main characters – the scene in which Tony and Susan return from their country weekend to find Barrett and Vera having sex in Tony's bedroom, the same room where the servant was first interviewed. Tony discovers his servants' sexual relationship while he stands on the stairs. From the bedroom door above, Barrett's silhouette looms on the wall in the background between Susan and Tony, marking the first of many triangular compositions (Figure 14). Once Tony demands that Barrett come downstairs, the confrontation, which reveals that Vera is not Barrett's sister, but his fiancée, and that Tony has had his own sexual encounters with her, features a particularly suggestive use of mirror images. Standing to the left of the convex mirror, Susan is, significantly, excluded from its reflection. Positioned in the center of the direct shots of Susan and Tony is the mirror itself, which first holds the distorted reflections of Tony and Barrett and, subsequently, when Vera arrives to announce her engagement to Barrett and declare that Tony "can't 'ave it on a plate for ever," frames and implicates the three occupants of the house. The figures in the convex mirror are foreshortened, diminished, and elongated like the eerie images in a carnival house of horrors.

Once Barrett and Vera are banished, the discourse takes a decisive turn, not only in terms of the story, but in style as well; for the film's last section is increasingly expressionist in its images and steadily more extreme in the characters' actions. To some extent the visual style of the later scenes is anticipated in details such as the distorted mirror images. Also the action and dialogue in the last section may be prefigured, as Losey intended, in the stylized tone of the restaurant and Mountset country house scenes earlier in the film. Both of these aspects are problematic, however, and a number

Figure 13. The distorted reflection in a convex mirror conveys the triangular relationships that pervade *The Servant*. (Courtesy Weintraub Entertainment Ltd.)

Figure 14. Tony and Susan discover that Barrett (in silhouette) and Vera (off screen) have usurped the master's bedroom for their sexual games. (Courtesy Weintraub Entertainment Ltd.)

Figure 15. A shadowy vortex, the stairway is a playground for the ball game and the many other power games between master and servant. (Courtesy Weintraub Entertainment Ltd.)

of critics have taken exception to them – ranging from Alexander Walker's modest caveat that the film is "very nearly" of a piece to American critic Vernon Young's conclusion that the shift is fatal to the film's unity. Young, who saw the film in the Venice festival and attended a press conference Losey gave afterward, referred to Losey's "defending the catastrophe which some few of us insisted had overtaken [*The Servant*]... at about the two-thirds mark" (1972, 223). One need not wholly agree with Young's severe judgment to conclude that the striking change in the last section threatens to undermine the film's overall coherence.

That Losey himself was concerned about the risk of disparate styles is clear from the story he told in various interviews about the rewriting of the restaurant scene. "Near the end of the shooting," he told Ciment:

I suddenly realized that the country house scene and the ball game scene were so stylized that in the existing material there were two different styles. The basis of one of the styles was in those two scenes, which took place at the beginning and near the end. The whole thing was going to break in two unless I had another sequence of that style

53

in the middle. So I called Harold and said to him that it could be done in the scene in the restaurant which originally was not a very good one because it was a very long dialogue scene between James Fox and Wendy Craig. It was uninterrupted, and not interesting. I felt that somehow the upper-class aspect of the country house and of the ball game required in the middle a kind of return to this society which, after all, was the background and basis of the picture. (1985, 227–8)

Although, interestingly, Losey misremembers the order (the restaurant scene precedes the country house and ball game scenes rather than occurring between them), his perceived need for balancing highly stylized scenes with the tone of the rest of the narration is perceptive.

A brief look at the Mountset country house scene, which caricatures an insular, moribund aristocracy, suggests what gave rise to Losey's concern. Tony tells Susan in the restaurant that Agatha and Willy Mountset have invited them for a weekend in the country. A long, leisurely pan of the gardens of the country estate to the accompaniment of sprightly, almost comic, music introduces the scene. Cutting to a shot inside the grand house, the camera follows a servant carrying drinks into a large formal room. The doors open as if onto a stage where the Mountsets and Tony and Susan are posed in a tableau. Behind each of the Mountsets stands marble statuary that seems to mock their stilted behavior (Figure 12). The subject matter and inflated tone of the conversation constitute a satire on both the self-assured ignorance of the Mountsets (Lady Mountset assures the others that South American cowboys are called "ponchos") and on Tony's naively idealistic and ludicrous plans to build cities in the Brazilian jungle. This amusing and theatrical send-up ends, aptly enough, with the exit of the servant and the closing of the doors that first opened onto the scene.

In the rewritten version of the restaurant scene, the counterpointed conversation between Tony and Susan arguing about Barrett nearly succeeds in subsuming the odd, seemingly irrelevant snatches of conversation of three other couples: a society man and woman, a bishop and his curate, and two apparent lesbians. That the latter two of these "overheard" conversations are rather nakedly about power, a frequent theme for Losey and Pinter and a major issue in *The Servant*, contributes to integrating them into the narrative overall. In addition, the scene is also intercut with brief shots of Barrett meeting Vera at the station and bringing her to Tony's house, which creates an ironic counterpoint to Tony's spirited defense of Barrett to the more mistrusting and discerning Susan and implies a connection between these otherwise separate events.

In addition to the shifts in tone and style, the last section of the film, for all the brilliance of individual moments, does not embrace the range of thematic possibilities that have emerged so much as set them out one by one. Viewed in the aggregate, the scenes following Tony's rehiring of Barrett are alternately realistic, parodic, surreal, and even allegorical, and they threaten to go in several directions (from homosexuality to a satiric inversion of the British class system to a Faustian version of evil) in offering possible explanations for the characters' motivations and precipitous slide into decadence. Interestingly, these scenes are rooted in the least explicit portion of Robin Maugham's novella. Maugham's first-person narrator, Richard Merton, who is omitted from the film, explains that he was spending a year in the United States during the period of Barrett's final ascendance to complete power over Tony. (The bare fact of Barrett's return has been mentioned to him in letters.) Merton says:

> I fear that the weakness of this story is that I am unable to explain the reason for the increase in Barrett's influence during the year I was away. He stood for ease and comfort in Tony's mind. But it must have been more than that. . . . Tony was lonely. The screen of convention which stood between him and Barrett had been shattered. There was now an easy understanding. They had been after the same girl. They were no longer master and servant. . . . Barrett was far too clever to state the position as baldly as I have done. I expect he took on his role as dragoman step by step, with sly little hints and furtive allusions, until he finally established his position as the agent who satisfied Tony's needs. (1964, 75–6)

Obviously, Losey and Pinter could not settle for anything so vague as the speculations and disclaimers offered by Maugham's narrator. Instead, the period of ascendancy is largely omitted in favor of portraying its consequences, which are startling in their departure from what has come before. Drawing on details from the novella – Barrett's and Tony's preoccupation with crossword puzzles, for example, and a final scene in which a teenage prostitute arrives while Merton is trying to make a last appeal to Tony – the film narrates the final collapse.

The last section begins with a scene of Tony working a crossword puzzle when Barrett, complaining of "all this muck and slime," sweeps into the room whose disarray contrasts with the self-conscious orderliness he earlier presided over. Tony, in a listless insistence on maintaining at least the appearance of proprieties between master and servant, responds: "Well, do something about it. You're supposed to be the bloody servant!" Barrett ignores this, replying that he is "not used to working in such squalor." He complains: "Look, why don't you get yourself a job instead of moping around here all day? Here I am scraping and skimping to make ends meet ...getting worse and worse...and you're no bloody help...d'you know that butter's gone up two-pence a pound?" As a set piece (despite the curious question of what has become of Tony's fortune) the scene works as an energetic satire of the reversal that now characterizes their relationship. But the changes are especially unsettling in the way they violate one's understanding of the characters. Moreover, placed at the beginning of this section, the particular shift in the characterizations of Tony and Barrett in this scene is likely to skew one's response to the following scenes that prepare for the darker, more decadent extremes of the conclusion.

Although Tony is not greatly changed as the listless and slovenly aristocrat, his ready acceptance of Barrett's crabbed and insolent speech is disconcerting, but not wholly implausible. Barrett, on the other hand, has become a bitchy, frazzled housemate who complains about everything from the price of butter to Tony's lack of employment. What has happened to the fastidious, controlled, and shrewdly manipulative man who dominates the first two-thirds of the film? Barrett is not just changed, but seems a parody of an upper-class notion of a frustrated working-class housewife. He has never been so stridently affected and almost effeminate as he is now in his open abuse of Tony. How to account for such a sudden and radical change in the servant, in his relationship with Tony, and in their general living conditions? Is one to assume that this petulant nag is the "real" Barrett whose hidden character is now revealed? Has living with Tony perhaps corrupted a trim and orderly Barrett who is weaker or more easily influenced than might be supposed from his past? While pointing to the problem, such explanations fail to convince. More important, beginning the section with a nagging "wife and husband" risks foregrounding homosexuality as reductively explanatory. To its credit, the film is more honest in facing the homosexual implications of the relationship than Maugham's novella, which never openly acknowledges the possibility, but this scene founders on caricature. Alternative interpretations involving the will to power and class conflict, as well as ambiguous sexuality, that the first two-thirds of the film kept viable and subtly balanced can hardly coexist if one believes what one sees and hears in the bickering of the two main characters, who have been, until now, beyond stereotyping.

The misbegotten nature of the squabbling-couple scene is the more obvious when it is compared with a slightly later scene in which Tony and Barrett, both dressed in coats and ties, have a dinner prepared by Barrett, which Tony declares "fabulous." Tony's compliments and Barrett's coy expressions of gratitude ("It's nice to know it's appreciated. It makes all the difference") certainly reveal the reversal that has taken place. Besides signaling at least a version of decorum, however oddly enacted, the scene hints at the possibile emergence of a latent homosexuality without relying on sex-role stereotypes. The most telling element arises in an exchange about friendships in both men's army days. Barrett says, "You know, sometimes I get the feeling that we're old pals." Tony responds, "That's funny . . . I get the same feeling myself." Barrett tells Tony that he has felt this way only once before, in the army. "That's funny," Tony again responds. "I had the same feeling myself there, too. Once." The reiteration of the word "once" subtly extends the possible sexual implications of the conversation and effectively suggests one aspect of the struggle for power between the two men. Interestingly, no other scene in this section has so quiet, almost poignant a tone, as if beyond the overt bickering and menacing contests, there might reside ordinary human frailty. But the moment is at best a truce, and the outcome of the violent games that ensue has more to do with power than mere victory.

From the almost conventional contest for dominance that marks the succeeding scene when Tony awakens Barrett and angrily insists that he clean up tea dregs on the carpet, the narrative moves to one of its most brilliant moments. Tony and Barrett, stationed on the staircase, play a ball game in which, as Pinter describes it in the screenplay, "according to their own rules, the ball must be bounced off the wall or on the stairs past the opponent" (1971, 50). Power, place, advantage all are at stake as the contestants revel at one moment in a point scored and protest in the next that they are being unfairly treated. Although Losey regarded this scene as one of the two whose style threatened to unbalance the film, it has little in common with either the restaurant or Mountset scenes. Nor is its narration extreme or divergent from the pattern of expressionism that grows steadily as the film approaches the orgy scene with which it concludes. In fact, the visual stylization is especially effective, genuinely enlarging the scene rather than merely calling attention to itself. In the images, there are, in a sense, four players in the game, for behind Barrett and Tony their shadows loom on the wall like phantom opponents, larger, insubstantial, but commanding, as if the shadow contest were the truer picture of the conflict (Figure 15). Barrett, who starts the game in the inferior position, will end up standing at the top of the stairs, where he dominates Tony (and the image), ordering Tony to run off and pour him a brandy.

That Barrett has ascended to full power over Tony is confirmed in the

Figure 16. The "Faust" scene where the Mephistophelian Barrett dominates the stuporous Tony. (Courtesy Weintraub Entertainment Ltd.)

formidable game of hide-and-seek they soon play. In the darkened house Barrett searches for Tony, calling to him in a voice no less sinister than it is soft and seductive. "Puss, puss, puss," Barrett coos. Tony's dread of being found (and found out, as suggested by Barrett's line while he stalks him, "You've got a guilty secret") is revealed in lurid images of the shifting shadows of Tony's face distorted on the shower curtain behind which he cowers in obvious terror (Figure 17). When at last Barrett tears back the curtain to expose Tony, one sees the faucet dripping just as the kitchen tap did in the scene when Vera seduced Tony. That Barrett's seduction of Tony is partly sexual is surely implied by the recurring image of dripping water, but the scene's disturbing power is darker and more malevolent than mere sexual seduction, however morally forbidden or socially condemned. The ruthless but recognizable power struggle of the ball game has been succeeded by something more amorphous, more far-reaching and dangerous, for in the hide-and-seek scene Barrett's dominance seems nearly demonic and Tony's will has collapsed, leaving him only a trembling victim. Not merely power, but evil itself seems to possess the house and its inhabitants.

Although Losey expressed regret at having once said *The Servant* was about Faust, because "this was a terrible over-simplification" (Milne 1968, 131), one of the most important scenes leading up to the orgy, and defining

Figure 17. In the ominous, almost surreal images of the hide-and-seek game, the shower curtain behind which Tony cowers distorts his shadowed profile. (Courtesy Weintraub Entertainment Ltd.)

Figure 18. Tony's magnified eye, seen through a glass sphere, in turn sees a misshapen, inverted world in the orgy scene that concludes the film. (Courtesy Weintraub Entertainment Ltd.)

the film's final darkness, strongly evokes the Faust legend. With a fire in the grate as background, a medium close-up of a tabletop shows a game of solitaire in progress. From the right margin of the frame, Barrett's hand moves the cards around and then places a small bottle of some liquid on the table as he is heard offering "something special" to the unseen Tony. Although he twice rather feebly rejects the potion, Tony succumbs to Barrett's inveigling to "just have a little sip." The camera draws back to a medium long shot of the two men, Barrett, at center right of the image, dominating Tony, who sits to the left on the floor virtually at Barrett's feet. "You see. I can still think of things that will please you, can't I?" says the tempter, as he pours yet another glass of the special concoction for Tony. The fire, the potion, and Barrett's superior solicitude all link him to the legendary Mephistopheles, particularly the versions of Marlowe and Goethe, as does Barrett's most Mephistophelean line to Tony, "My only ambition is to serve you. You know that, don't you?" (Figure 16). Even Barrett's strategy of admitting mistakes recalls Mephistopheles' tactics, and Barrett's excuse to Tony – "After all, I'm only human, aren't I? You wouldn't like me if I wasn't human, would you?" – hints at the question of the servant's almost preternatural, if not diabolical, personality. Tony, too, in his pathetic struggle to articulate a plan of action, enacts a tortured version of Faust's striving that, in Goethe's drama at least, defines man's restless spirit and insatiable curiosity, a striving that eventually saves Faust's soul. In a painfully halting manner, Tony says to Barrett: "Listen . . . Listen . . . Perhaps . . . we . . . could both . . . make . . . an extra effort." With a snap of his fingers and a patronizing slap to Tony's cheek, Barrett replies: "You're right, Tony, you're dead right. That's what we ought to do." The deadly sins are by now obvious in the film – pride, envy, anger, greed, lust, and especially sloth. Like Mephistopheles, Barrett takes possession of Tony's life and soul by playing the procurer for his desires. Unlike Faust, however, Tony is not stirred to activity; he is not defined or saved by his striving, but damned by his sloth.

The difficulties centering on consistency of characterization, stylistic coherence, and structural unity that grow pronounced in the scenes after Barrett's return persist through the orgy scene that ends the film. Among the most obvious inconsistencies is Susan's character. Angry and offended by what she learned when Tony, both shamed and betrayed, ordered Barrett and Vera from the house, Susan walked out on Tony. Reappearing now, Susan seems an entirely different character – passive, uncertain, even submissive, where previously she was opinionated and assertive in defending Tony and her own social status against Barrett's encroachments. In this last scene Susan, a most unlikely advocate of Vera's needs and rights, even urges a nearly incoherent Tony to pay Vera some recompense for his past misuse of her. In addition, Susan abases herself, kissing Barrett and then submitting to Barrett's kisses and his taunts in a desperate last attempt (according to Losey's own explanation of her motivations) to rouse Tony and incite him to defend her. Her actions, however, are unconvincing and out of character; only when she slaps Barrett as he shows her out the door does she slip back into or reclaim her previously defined character.

More than inconsistencies of characterization or stylistic excesses have troubled some critics, who have found the orgy scene marred by empty or too explicit allegorizing. Nonetheless, Losey, who could be both an astute and a harsh critic of his own work, steadfastly defended the ending. "Personally I *like* the orgy scene," he told Tom Milne. "I like the film, and I couldn't have made it any other way at the time" (1968, 136). Losey also defended the orgy to Ciment and argued as well for the coherence of the other highly stylized scenes: "A lot of people said, at the time, that the orgy was tacked on and it wasn't the same picture – which is not true. There was a direct development out of the country house, the restaurant, the ball game, to the orgy" (1985, 231). Although Losey can rightly point to preceding scenes that establish a stylized mode of presentation, few similarities can be drawn between the orgy and the country house and restaurant scenes. The latter are sharply satiric – witty and shrewd, even savage, but not ominous and disturbing. By contrast, the ominous scenes, those most charged with menace, the Faust and hide-and-seek scenes, together with the ball game scene, do prepare for the fateful ending by presenting not merely a reversal of the master–servant roles, but the collapse of all social norms and moral values in a world where all barriers are down.

Losey's view of the orgy scene suggests the extent to which he intended to subvert one's distance from the film's world. The "sequence is uneasy," he wrote, "It's uncomfortable, because it turns people back on themselves ... makes them face up to certain things that are implicit in the preceding material" (1970, 59). Clearly he intends the scene not only as a conclusion, but as a formal closure of the overall design of the narration, which, ironically, exploits ambiguity to make explicit the nightmare of dissolution that is implicit from the beginning. In the orgy scene Tony's complete collapse, narcotized finally to the point of stupor, and Barrett's malevolent stage managing of a strangely shapeless but devouring decadence reach a surreal climax that is genuinely disturbing in its shadowy and ambiguous details. Like the house itself, the film is hermetically sealed, reflexive in the narcissistic images of characters gazing into mirrors or through glass balls that distort and invert the already bizarre interior world (Figure 18). Thus, Tony and Vera (who, having sought to return to the house only to be banished, is inexplicably present once again) point a camera at a mirror, taking a snapshot of their own reflection. In a sense the film implodes; the house clock, whose chimes have regularly sounded at the most dramatic moments, stops; and Tony, immobilized by drugs and drink, slips into a timeless world under Barrett's control.

However controversial its extremes, the conclusion of *The Servant* remains at least an arguable closure of its tale of the darkness that has invaded the world of the house and the characters who seal themselves off within it. Whatever one's judgment of the orgy scene, ambiguity is likely to be at issue, for it is crucial to the film not just in its conclusion but throughout. In an interview Pinter once said:

> I do so hate the becauses of drama. Who are we to say that this happens because that happened, that one thing is a consequence of another? ... The most we know for sure is that the things which have happened have happened in a certain order: any connections we think we see, or choose to make, are pure guesswork. Life is much more mysterious than plays make it out to be. And it is this mystery which fascinates me. (Klein 1985, 51)

Although Pinter's remarks about the "becauses" were in response to questions about *Accident,* they are equally relevant to *The Servant* with its troubling question of causality. Just why did this particular moral catastrophe happen? For that matter, was it moral, social, or psychological? Was it the inevitable product of a historical dialectic, as Alexander Walker observes, or, more narrowly, the psychological intersection of two personalities, each with his own weaknesses, merely waiting for some fatal invitation? Or do the social forces and individual frailties constitute the terms for enacting an allegory of the triumph of evil where good has abdicated its place? Not surprisingly, the film has produced wide-ranging disagreements about the answers to these questions.

Calling *The Servant* "the definitive Losey film," Gordon Gow observed that it "has been variously construed as a class-struggle metaphor, an essay on the ascendency urge, a study of evil. All definitions seem to me valid" (1971, 37). Alexander Walker cites still more disparate interpretations: " 'The parable of a man and his *alter ego*' (Richard Roud, the *Guardian*); 'Is it, by implication, a study of homosexuality?' (Eric Rhode, the *Listener*);

'a film about possession, not merely who owns what but who owns who [*sic*]' (Philip Oakes, the *Sunday Telegraph*); 'an all-out attack on Britain's caste system' (*Time*)" (1974, 218). Walker's view, like Gow's, is that the richness of the film's metaphoric treatment of the master–servant relationship contains a multiplicity of meanings. This is certainly true, but the disagreements about interpretation can also be traced to the shift in style and characterizations once the servant is taken back by the master who fired him in the first place, and even more precisely, to the weight of the first scene after Barrett's return, when the themes of sexual identity and power are treated in such broad terms.

At its best *The Servant* reveals and prefigures what *Accident* and *The Go-Between* later confirm and extend: the singular vision shared by Losey and Pinter involves mystery. Not suspense, but mystery. Not a lack of causes but an obsession with consequences dominates all three of their collaborations. The "why" that haunts *The Servant* is not irrelevant, but neither is it the reason for telling the story. Indeed, as its many and varied interpretations suggest, there is no shortage of plausible explanations of the calamity the film narrates. Losey, like Pinter, is drawn to the mystery of human behavior and motivation precisely because it is mysterious, finally unexplainable. As early as *Time Without Pity*, where the identity of the murderer is revealed in the first scene of what would otherwise be a conventional whodunit, Losey rejected mere suspense. In *Accident* and *The Go-Between* Losey and Pinter explore one of the most perplexing questions about human behavior: not why such things happen but what it means that they have happened.

For these filmmakers, seeing life whole means confronting and accepting its ambiguity rather than imposing explanations. But there is no gainsaying that ambiguity is always a calculated risk in narrative, where it can exceed the richness of unresolved but suggestive possibilities earned by a text to slip into what amounts only to frustrating uncertainty or obscurantism. In the final analysis *The Servant*, despite its considerable strengths, is vulnerable on these grounds. Indeed, Losey agreed when Milne observed that "there is a stage missing" in the film (1968, 137). Losey's distinction between suspense and mystery, however, along with Pinter's view of causality, point to the demanding rewards of narratives that do not simply offer answers to questions. Questions more than answers, consequences more compelling than their causes – these are the stuff of the films Losey and Pinter have made together. First in *The Servant* and then in the more complex and fully realized *Accident* and *The Go-Between*, they make clear that there can be no other way of telling a story they find worth telling.

4

"The Inner Violence"

Accident

The rich command of his medium and deepening understanding of the themes of power and privilege that are evident in *King and Country* and *The Servant* anticipate Losey's more ambitious achievements in *Accident*. The heightened tension between evocative imagery and understated language that pervades the first of Losey's collaborations with Harold Pinter is even more striking in their second film together, which was adapted from a novel by Nicholas Mosley. Similarly, the intensely personal revelation of character that marks the story of Hamp and Hargreaves is also at work. Compared with these earlier films, however, the world of *Accident* seems almost uneventful except for the fatal accident with which the film begins; there are no conflicts as overt as the court-martial or the corrupt struggle between master and servant. Instead, destructive contests are masked by calm surfaces profoundly at odds with concealed passions. Beneath the restrained, civilized forms of English university life, passion and power prove indivisible; sexual desire and deception compel moves and countermoves whereby advantage is secretly won or lost. The tension between what is spoken and what unspoken, between what is desired and what denied is made palpable by a narration in which, as Pinter described it, "everything happens, nothing is explained.... Just a level, intense look at people, at things. As though if you look at them hard enough they will give up their secrets" (Taylor 1966, 184). The result is a remarkably suggestive film in which there always seems more at stake than either the characters or the narration openly acknowledge.

The first-person narrator of Nicholas Mosley's novel says, "Once this would have been a thing of tension; bells and music. Now we act it all so slowly. The camera stays for minutes on a close-up. Speaks for itself. Silence. Time running out" (1967, 46). The passage is notable not only for its cinematic allusion, but more importantly for the way it joins two kinds or levels of subjectivity: the narrator's remembered experience and his narrational act of remembering. In Mosley's complex handling of point of view, objective reality is twice removed. The narrator presents his memories, which are inherently fragmentary and associative, and their substance is not so much the original events as it is his subjective experience: the events occurred; the narrator *as a character* experienced them; and that experience is in turn remembered and narrated. In the novel, then, the process of narration is at least as important as the narrative it produces, for the consciousness of the first-person narrator – his intellect, emotions, and values, and their subjective interaction – dominates the story he tells. Both the novel's events and characters, including the narrator himself, can be said to have no existence apart from the act of recollection. Implicitly, of course, this is the case in all first-person narratives, but Mosley foregrounds the subjectivity, making it the narration's defining trait and a theme as well. This "rather extraordinary free association novel," Losey told Michel Ciment, "seemed to me ideal material and so it did to Harold" (1985, 259). From the Mosley book there "came a much more free collaboration and a much closer, much more exciting and interesting one because of the way we both saw the use of film" (239–40).

"We thought a lot about how it should be done, and worked together very closely on it," Pinter remarked.

> At first we thought of perhaps trying to do it the way the book does, to find a direct film equivalent to the free-association, stream-of-consciousness style of the novel. I tried a draft that way, but it just wouldn't work.... Do exactly the same thing on film and the result is precious, self-conscious, overelaborate. (Taylor 1966, 183)

Forsaking the novel's style, however, did not mean forsaking subjectivity altogether. Rather, it meant turning to a different mode, that of "art-cinema" narration with its potential for complex relationships between objectivity and subjectivity, rather than classical narration, which typically relies on observable reality as an index of characters' inner lives. "I wanted to make a film about an accident in which there was no physical violence," Losey said, "only the inner violence of what people feel" (Milne 1968, 19). In the film that Losey and Pinter would make of *Accident,* a simple, unadorned look at the characters and their physical world would discover surfaces intended not to reveal, but to deceive. "In this film everything is buried," Pinter said. "The drama goes on inside the characters" (Taylor 1966, 184), and that is precisely the realm of the subjective.

Unlike the novel, the film begins and ends in time-present, which frames a long time-past section (fully two-thirds of the running time) and raises the fundamental question of whether the two time frames are narrated by the same voice. Is there, as some critics have maintained, an overall omniscient narration that produces the "objective" reality of the present and also the "expressive" or subjective reality of the central character's memories of time-past? Or is the past narrated by the character himself? If the latter, does the omniscient narration's potential for commentary continue during the character-narration of the past, or is it suspended until the resumption of time-present? Is there one narrational commentary or two?[1] If two — the character's and that of the omniscient narration — are their commentaries during time-past simultaneous or discrete, at one narrational level or two? These questions, which turn on the possibilities of subjectivity in film, require close attention, for the source and nature of the film's moral judgment is centrally at issue. In the novel judgment clearly belongs to the first-person narrator; is the same true of the film? And in light of this question what is the importance of the relationship of character-narration to characterization? One can argue that character is most expressively revealed in action, and it would be a mistake to suppose that Losey and Pinter reject this view altogether. The "level, intense look at people, at things" argues otherwise. Instead, they enlarge the concept of action to include a character's own private, even secret, act of narrating that can be no less decisive for having occurred solely in the realm of subjective experience.

Accident's concern with the presentness of the past transforms a conventional tale of sexual passion and personal betrayal into a complex study of the nature of consciousness. In the interaction of third- and first-person voices, the film deals specifically with the reverberations of events in the inner life of the central character, and much of the inner life is narrated by the character himself in a long first-person sequence contained within a third-person time-present frame. Time, then, is not only a theme but also an organizing principle of both narration and characterization; for the sense of time's "ever-presentness" is a dimension of consciousness, a function of memory, which is more than a mere storehouse of recollections. That which is remembered is necessarily interpreted by the rememberer, who in this film is both a character and a narrator. Remembering, then, is itself an event, the *act* of narration, performed by a character within the discourse, and as such it is a singularly complex instance of self-revelation. The first-person narrator, who produces the time-past character and the events that engage him, is a version of the time-present character, albeit one not necessarily aware of the implications of all he narrates.

Accident's story centers on Stephen (Dirk Bogarde), a middle-aged Oxford don with a wife and children, who becomes obsessed with Anna (Jacqueline Sassard), a beautiful young Austrian woman who is his pupil. When he discovers that another of his pupils, William (Michael York), a young aristocrat, is romantically interested in Anna, and later that she is having an affair with his colleague and friend, Charley (Stanley Baker), also a married middle-aged don, Stephen enters an unacknowledged but fateful sexual competition. On the way to Stephen's house after a late-night party, William is killed in a car accident in which Anna was probably driving. After rescuing her from the wreckage, Stephen takes Anna to his house, where he virtually forces her to have sex with him. The next morning he drives her back to Oxford. Later that day, Stephen returns to Anna's room and watches, along with an uncomprehending Charley, while she packs and leaves. Afterwards, Stephen returns to his wife and children and the life he lived before the accident.

The discourse rearranges these events. Beginning at the time of the accident, it presents the story's events in chronological order for a while. Thus, Stephen rescues Anna and takes her to his house, where he seeks to comfort her and also telephones the police. When the police arrive, Stephen gives his brief account of the accident, but omits any mention of Anna. Afterward, Stephen goes upstairs, where he finds Anna sleeping fitfully. As he watches her, he sees her foot twitch and is reminded of the instant only moments earlier when, as he helped her from the overturned car in which William lay dead, he suddenly screamed: "Don't! You're standing on his face!" At this moment the discourse suspends the story's forward progress and returns to time-past, to its earliest narrated event, a scene in Stephen's room in college at Oxford on the summer day when he and William first spoke of Anna. The discourse then proceeds chronologically with the long time-past sequence of events that unfolded between that conversation with William and the afternoon some time later when Stephen last saw William and Anna at a cricket match only hours before the fatal accident. After the cricket match scene, the discourse returns to Stephen's memory of the image of William dead, then Anna climbing from the overturned car, and then to time-present where Stephen still stands watching Anna sleeping. This last transitional sequence reverses the path of the initial movement to time-past, and with the resumption of time-present, the discourse continues to follow the story's chronology to the conclusion.

At the moment when story and discourse diverge in *Accident,* the question of narration – that is, the identity of the narrator(s) – becomes significant, indeed decisive. A sequence of five shots effects the transition from time-present to time-past (more precisely, to two stages of time-past) and from the overall third-person narration to Stephen's character-narration or mind-screen (Figures 19–23). Considered individually, the shots seem simple, but they can be understood properly only in the context of the sequence as a whole. The five shots are as follows:

(1) Medium shot of Stephen looking out of the frame. [time-present]
(2) Medium shot from the waist down of Anna sleeping with one shoe off. Her foot twitches. [time-present]
(3) Close-up of Anna's foot kicking the shoe. [time-present]
(4) Close-up of Anna stepping on William's face in the wrecked car. (Stephen's off-screen voice is heard screaming: "Don't!") [recent time-past]
(5) Close-up of William's smiling face in Stephen's Oxford rooms. (Stephen's off-screen voice is heard asking: "You haven't spoken to her?" When William says "No," Stephen's off-screen voice continues: "You've just seen her.") [earlier time-past]

The relationship of shots (1) and (2) is the simplest, constituting a conventional pairing of third person and first whose code indicates that the camera momentarily presents Stephen's physical point of view as he looks at Anna (Figures 19–20). However, with (3), the close-up of Anna's foot kicking her shoe, which is very brief, the complexity increases substantially. This shot is the crucial one in the sequence. In one sense (3) constitutes a continuation of (2) in which Stephen saw Anna's foot involuntarily twitch, but the continuation is only temporal, not spatial, for camera angle and distance both change (Figure 21). The camera, therefore, can no longer be understood as temporarily occupying Stephen's physical vantage point as it was established in (1). Consequently, several possibilities arise. Has Stephen perhaps moved to another location? The extreme brevity of (3), the shot of Anna's foot kicking the shoe, makes that unlikely. Or has the third-person narration of (1) resumed? Possibly, but the next shot argues against that, for (4), the shot of Anna stepping on William's face, is certainly subjective, Stephen's involuntary recall of the recent past (Figure 22). One might argue that (3) is not subjective because the camera's angle and position do not conform to Stephen's physical perspective, but the case for subjectivity is confirmed by the dialogue. In the original time-present scene of the accident, Stephen shouted, "Don't! You're standing on his face!" In (4) he shouts only "Don't!" The change makes clear that while this is not a conventional point of view shot, neither is it merely a recapitulation by the third-person narration; rather, it is Stephen's (figurative) memory. Thus, given that (2), the shot of Anna sleeping, and (4), her stepping on William, are both subjective, and that (3), Anna's foot kicking the shoe, is both extremely brief and so intimately related to the object of (2), it is hardly plausible to consider the shot of her kicking the shoe as a momentary resumption of third-person narration that is almost instantly relinquished. That (3) is subjective has important implications for both narration and characterization.

If (3) is not Stephen's physical point of view, then, unlike (2), it is a form of character-narration, what Edward Branigan would distinguish as "character projection" and Bruce Kawin would call mindscreen.[2] In other words, (2) is subjective *camera*, a point of view shot; its field is the character's physical eye. The field of (3), however, is the mind's eye. The consequences of this distinction are crucial, for the field of the mind's eye is always a function of character-narration, whatever its duration. Moreover, character-narration expresses its narrator's interpretations, whether rational or irrational, voluntary or involuntary. The key issue is that shots (2) through (5) are all subjective, but in different ways. Thus, (2) is conventional subjective camera, or point of view, and (4) is mindscreen-memory. However, (3) is what Kawin (after Munsterberg) would explain as an "act of attention," and Branigan as character projection. This close-up is not anchored in Stephen's literal gaze but in his thoughts that motivate and define the camera's gaze. The discourse, then, moves from Stephen's physical view of Anna, to his momentary concentration on a detail, and on to his memory generated by that detail. The result is a subtle but discrete movement along a continuum of subjectivity more complex than that customarily recognized in narrative film. Considered in this context, (3) can now be recognized as not dependent on Stephen's physical position vis-à-vis Anna. Instead, the shot presents his mind's isolation of details – Anna's foot and shoe – that he associates with the earlier incident and that trigger his memory of it. Stephen is thus the *off-screen narrator* of both (3) and (4), which, given their relationship and their brevity, seem calculated to suggest the mental process of involuntary association.

With (5), the shot of William in Stephen's room in college, the discourse returns to the beginning of the story, or at least to its earliest narrated event (Figure 23). But (5) is not the first instance of time-past in the discourse, merely the earliest chronologically. The first instance is (4), Stephen's memory of Anna stepping on William in the wrecked car. Because (3) and (4) are both mindscreen, although of different kinds, it is clear when (5) immediately follows that Stephen's mind has turned swiftly from the dreadful memory of

Figure 19. An objective shot of Stephen looking at Anna asleep on his bed in *Accident*. (Courtesy Weintraub Entertainment Ltd.)

Figure 20. Anna seen from Stephen's point of view. (Courtesy Weintraub Entertainment Ltd.)

Figure 21. This subjective shot, Stephen's "act of attention" rather than his physical point of view, makes the transition to character-narration. (Courtesy Weintraub Entertainment Ltd.)

William dead (recent time-past) to this happier one (earlier time-past). The last three shots of the sequence all originate in Stephen's mind and reveal not only his association of discrete moments on the basis of some common detail, but, more importantly, his inclination to turn away from painful memories.

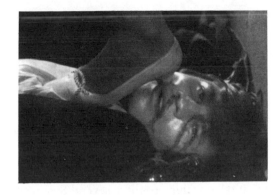

Figure 22. In his character-narration, Stephen's involuntary memory recalls the moment when Anna stepped on William's face. (Courtesy Weintraub Entertainment Ltd.)

Figure 23. Stephen's character-narration returns to the earliest time-past event, in which he and William converse in Stephen's room in college. (Courtesy Weintraub Entertainment Ltd.)

In terms of narration, the movement from recent to earlier time-past reflects a (perhaps unconscious) narrating strategy on Stephen's part. In effect, Stephen as first-person narrator adopts or appropriates a style usually associated with traditional third-person "objective" narration, a stance outside the narrated events. Ironically, Stephen's attempt to distance himself is both an avoidance and a form of implied self-judgment. As his own narration will eventually reveal, the displacing of traumatic memories with happier ones is not a wholly successful escape for Stephen. He may seek to evade or suppress certain unpleasant facts or feelings, but finally he cannot deny them. Revealed first in the movement from time-present to the two stages of time-past, this characteristic of Stephen's moral and psychological nature will prove decisive in the aftermath of his dark encounter with Anna.

The reasons for examining this short sequence at such length are, one hopes, now evident, for it is crucial to recognize that Stephen has several distinct existences within the film. He is a character in the discourse. He also narrates part of it. And these two Stephens are not identical. Simply put, in time-present he is an on-screen character produced by the overall third-person narration; in time-past he is the off-screen first-person narrator who produces still another on-screen character, the remembered Stephen who is this mindscreen narrator's self-conception. However similar (even apparently the same) these two characters named Stephen may be, they are nonetheless discrete. Moreover, neither of them is precisely the same as the Stephen who is a narrator. This means that even as one watches and responds immediately to the actions of the Stephen-character of time-past, one is simultaneously watching another event, the act of character-narration performed by the Stephen of time-present. Thus, the overall characterization is a function of the various potential relationships of these several Stephens and the formal means that produce them. What, then, is Stephen like? What does one know about him, and how does one know it?

The answers to these questions depend on an analysis of levels of narration, even though some critics have maintained that in *Accident* there is only one level – that of an omniscient narration that presents both time-present and time-past. In his book on Losey, Foster Hirsch compares the first-person narration of Mosley's novel with what he asserts is the "objective" third-person narration in the film:

> No longer is Stephen's consciousness the stage on which the action is set. Stephen appears in every scene in the film, but the events and characters are not filtered through his attitudes as Pinter makes no attempt to translate onto film the novel's Jamesian experiment in limited point of view. Quite the reverse of duplicating or of finding visual equivalents for the interior, increasingly subjective frame of the novel, Pinter presents the story and characters in a cool, objective manner – we are kept at a distance from all the characters, including Stephen. (1980, 119)

Seeing only one level of narration in *Accident*, Hirsch presents a reductive view of the film. One may not identify with Stephen in any approving or even sympathetic way, but neither is one "kept at a distance from all the characters, including Stephen." Hirsch acknowledges that the narrative is Stephen's, noting that Stephen "appears in every scene" (which is not precisely accurate), but the failure to see Stephen's function in the discourse as *narrator* surely robs the film of much of its psychological complexity.[3]

Viewing the entire discourse as third-person narration also leads to a decidedly dark assessment of Stephen's moral and emotional temperament.

Thus, for example, Beverle Houston and Marsha Kinder observe that, unlike the "highly sympathetic" character in Mosley's novel, the film's Stephen is cool, fearful, and devious. They see his "repressed and manipulating behavior" as revealing a "true opportunist," who is ultimately guilty of rape (1978, 28). This view is insightful as far as it goes – Stephen is indeed repressed and manipulative and often acts deviously – but the implications of character-narration need to be taken into account. The source of much of the information leading to this view is, in fact, the first-person narrator, who is a function (or aspect) of the Stephen of time-present. One must consider not only the time-past character's circumstances and behavior but Stephen-narrator's implied view or judgment of them as well, remembering always that both of these characterize the Stephen of time-present. The result is a character no more morally and emotionally justified than the one Houston and Kinder describe but, because of mindscreen, one who is different nonetheless. For the darker estimate of Stephen is implied by a narrator who is a larger version of the character himself. Because, as Seymour Chatman has pointed out, "the character-interpretive behavior of audiences is structured" (1978, 138), in *Accident* one must consider Stephen-narrator's role in characterization, for it is a unique element of that structuring. All of time-past, then, not just its events but all the details of its representation, can be read as revelatory of Stephen's psychological traits and moral nature.

Stephen's judgment is the more significant precisely because it remains private, confined to the realm of consciousness. He tells his tale to himself, not to another character – not even to the film's audience, which, in a manner of speaking, is eavesdropping. Thus, the mindscreen, Stephen's time-present view of his own past experience, is an instance of what Kawin would term "unauthorized narration," a kind of involuntary telling of his tale. The distinction between authorized and unauthorized narration is one of intention. Does the mindscreen narrator mean to tell his tale to listeners, however defined, or does he see himself as his only auditor?[4] Because Stephen's narration is intended only for himself (unlike, for example, Walter Neff's in *Double Indemnity* or, in a different mode, Jane Eyre in Robert Stevenson's film of Charlotte Bronte's novel), it is unauthorized and all the more revealing, for such narration is uncontaminated by the need to convince anyone other than the narrator himself.[5]

Unauthorized first-person narration, however, provides an especially strong possibility of discerning a simultaneous commentary by third-person narration as well. In *Accident* the view of Stephen inferable from the om-

niscient narration of the opening and closing time-present segments is sometimes evident in time-past also. (For most viewers, recognizing the interaction of the two levels is likely to be retrospective; i.e., the return to
omniscient narration at the conclusion of time-past reasserts its larger perspective, which can then be more readily traced in what has gone before.)
The ironic relationship of these levels of narration is particularly notable
in several key scenes. In the first, Stephen returns to his room in college
immediately after falling into the river while punting with William and Anna.
Significantly, the narration includes the sound of his fall, but excludes the
physical action itself, removing it to the realm of off-screen space. This
narrational ploy is consistent with Stephen's ongoing efforts to turn away
from disturbing facts, a personal inclination that has been evident since the
original movement from time-present to time-past. Moreover, the view of
both instances of evasion can be seen as expressing a degree of insight into
Stephen's character that may exceed his own understanding; a judgment by
the overall omniscient narration is thus strongly suggested.

Once he recovers from his angry embarrassment and changes into dry
clothes, Stephen sits on a couch with William sharing whiskey and talking
with easy familiarity. In his exploitation of time and space (including eli-
sions), Stephen as mindscreen narrator implicitly interprets the remembered
incident. The conversation focuses on his apprehensions about growing old,
his assertion that aristocrats are "made to be killed" (to which William
replies, "Of course, they're immortal"), and his suggestion that William
bring Anna to his house on Sunday. Given what eventually happens, this
conversation seems not only psychologically revealing but very nearly prescient, and certainly ironic. Interestingly, between the scene's first two segments – that is, after Stephen's lament about aging and before his exchange
with William about aristocrats – a cut to an exterior view of the college
shows gargoyles on a building's facade while a bell is heard tolling four
o'clock. A second cut returns to the room, and the conversation resumes.
Moments later, after Stephen's remark about the fate of aristocrats, another
cut shows the exterior view again, and the bell is now heard tolling five
o'clock just as William is heard making his reply about immortality. Obviously, neither exterior shot presents Stephen's physical point of view.
Rather, they are best understood as belonging to both levels of narration:
a figurative image (character projection) in Stephen's case, and an implied
commentary in the case of the omniscient narration, which recognizes the
irony and places the conversation and events in the larger context of the
discourse overall. Also, the two instances of the clock's tolling, which occur

during the scene, not at each end of it, indicate conclusively that the conversation is a good deal longer than the portion actually narrated. Whatever the full extent of the conversation, Stephen-narrator (along with the omniscient narration) has distilled the essence of the occasion in linking the subjects of aging, William's fate, and the then fledgling obsession with Anna. The irony could not have been apparent to Stephen at the time, of course, but it is now inescapable to the character-narrator who is remembering, as it is to the third-person narration as well. The interpretive emphases dispel any possibility of seeing even this early stage of events as merely coincidental. Motives and designs, however unacknowledged at the time by Stephen's conscious mind, were at work even then.

Shortly after the scene with William, the narration presents the only scene in which Stephen is not present as a character – a scene not included in the published version of Pinter's screenplay. Just after Stephen has told his wife Rosalind (Vivien Merchant) about inviting William and Anna to Sunday lunch, there is a cut to a scene showing the lone Charley, carrying a bottle of liquor and some papers, entering Stephen's room at Oxford. Charley lights a cigarette, glances over some books and papers on Stephen's desk, and tosses his burned match into the fireplace. Other than its position in the discourse – that is, after Stephen announces the invitation to lunch and before the Sunday sequence itself – there is no indication of this scene's place in the story's chronology. Neither is there any explanation of how Stephen-narrator knows of this event. On these grounds, one might argue that third-person narration intervenes to show us what Stephen obviously cannot see. Or one might argue that Stephen's narration includes information he learned after the fact – by Charley telling him, for example. Certainly nothing precludes character-narration from including such details. An interesting and even more suggestive explanation – one not inconsistent with Kawin's notion of mindscreen or Branigan's of character projection, nor with simultaneous levels of narration – is that the scene is an imagined, not an actual, event. In other words, according to this interpretation, the scene is produced by neither a third-person narration with greater knowledge than the character nor the character's own reconstructing memory alone. Instead, generated by Stephen's envy, jealousy, and suspicion of Charley, the scene metaphorically expresses Stephen's psychological state, his sense that Charley constantly encroaches on his territory. Mindscreen (like character projection) can be motivated by and can express a character's state of mind; when in the very next scene Charley arrives uninvited at Stephen's house for Sunday lunch, he is carrying items (liquor and this time a newspaper) that appear to link these two intrusions with Stephen's fear that Charley's presence invades his entire life.

In the most famous sequence in the film (nearly one-quarter of its screen time) the character-narrator presents the Sunday afternoon on which William and Anna and the uninvited Charley spend the day with Stephen and Rosalind. Still unaware of Charley's affair with Anna, Stephen is at first merely dismayed by his colleague's insistent and distracting presence. Nonetheless, the sunny, apparently tranquil day unfolds with seductive languor as the characters have lunch, play tennis, have conversations, and go for walks. Eventually, despite Rosalind's pregnancy and her obvious coolness to the idea, Stephen invites the visitors to stay for supper. If on its surface the afternoon is unremarkable, the narration reveals a level of unacknowledged tension and a veiled sexual sparring, principally between Stephen and Charley, that leave Rosalind wary and William a vaguely confused bystander.

The deceptively casual, languid scene on the lawn in the midst of the Sunday sequence is in many ways a paradigm of reflexive storytelling, again suggesting a commentary at the omniscient level, for the scene contains a series of stories within stories. The first of the scene's twenty-one shots is a high-angle shot that zooms back from wine decanters on the grass to encompass Stephen's family and guests on the lawn. The dialogue between William and Charley that begins in the second shot presents storytelling as the overtly reflexive subject of the scene. Charley, who is a novelist, tells William, who would like to write a novel but believes he cannot, that writing is easy – "It's child's play." Charley encourages William to become a storyteller – "Here on this lawn . . . what are we all up to?" – but another story briefly intervenes as Stephen's daughter, Clarissa, tells Anna about the trip she and her mother will make on Tuesday to Grandma's house, where Rosalind will rest during the last weeks of her pregnancy. At its simplist level, storytelling is "child's play," stringing together one event after another in the same way that Anna, in the foreground of the second shot, makes a daisy chain of flowers, a necklace she places on Clarissa as the scene concludes. With Clarissa's brief story completed, Charley, putting on his glasses (a kind of emblem of his perception and control), again asks William to "describe what we're all doing" (Figure 24).

William's story is a simple description of the immediate scene. His straightforward, unimaginative account of the people around him isolates the characters in their discrete activities ("Rosalind is lying down. Stephen is weeding the garden. Anna's making a daisy chain. We're having this conversation"). Reasserting his storytelling role, Charley points out to William that "you could go further." Shots (11) through (15), including the dialogue, are as follows:

(11) (medium shot of Rosalind) CHARLEY: Rosalind is pregnant.
(12) (two-shot of William and Charley with Stephen gardening in the background) CHARLEY: Stephen is having an affair with a girl at Oxford.
(13) (reaction shot of Anna) CHARLEY: He's reached the age when he can't keep his hands off...
(14) (reaction shot, medium close-up of Stephen and the first shot to isolate him in the scene) CHARLEY: ...girls at Oxford.
(15) (two-shot of William and Charley) CHARLEY: But he feels guilty, of course, so he makes up a story.
    WILLIAM: What story?
    CHARLEY: This story.
    WILLIAM: What are you talking about?

Several points concerning storytelling, characterization, and irony need elaborating here. In addition to the reflexivity of the dialogue that foregrounds storytelling and stories, the scene is resonant with ironies generated by knowledge held by and withheld from various characters. First, William proves to be a rather naive spectator and listener, nonplussed by Charley's tale, particularly its odd and reflexive conclusion. Charley tells a story, which he ascribes to the silent Stephen, in much the same way that Stephen, as character-narrator of time-past, is the off-screen narrator of this scene. Charley, of course, is the on-screen teller of this story within a story, and unbeknownst to anyone in the scene but himself and Anna (note shot (13) of the knowing Anna), he is telling his own story, for the viewer later learns that he and Anna are already engaged in an affair that the married and guilt-ridden Charley is projecting onto Stephen. As a character within the scene, Stephen knows nothing of Charley's affair or the full irony of Charley's projection onto him, although both Stephen's and Rosalind's reactions to Charley's story may well indicate their anxieties surrounding Stephen's attraction to Anna. When Stephen acknowedges that he has overheard Charley's story, he proves to be, unlike William, a far more knowing target, smarting from the psychological accuracy of this displaced story. Whether Charley has fortuitously or knowingly hit on Stephen's private obsession is uncertain, but he is undoubtedly a shrewd and manipulative player in the personal, sexual, and professional competition that characterizes his rela-

77

Figure 24. Charley, who encourages William to "describe what we're all doing here," will shortly narrate a story projecting his own affair with Anna onto Stephen. (Courtesy Weintraub Entertainment Ltd.)

tionship with Stephen. Beyond Charley's rather transparent intent to shock, the full irony of his story is delayed (for Stephen-character and for the viewer) until Stephen finds Charley and Anna using his house a few days later.

Although the scene on the lawn includes several storytellers of varying sophistication – Clarissa, William, and Charley – its presentation belongs to Stephen-narrator. The editing in the scene, for example, particularly when Charley relates Stephen's putative affair with one of the "girls at Oxford," seems motivated by Charley's story, withholding shots of Stephen until Charley verbalizes his friend's sexual fantasy/escapade. However much this effectively reinforces Charley's storytelling, it remains for the ironic, knowing, and judging mindscreen narrator to focus on the remembered surprise and guilt Stephen felt when he was caught in Charley's net. In these rapidly shifting and subtly composed images, the character-narrator "sees" himself in his ambiguous, even dishonest relationships with these characters. Rosalind, for instance, has a variable place in this memory, more often in its background or at its margins, but unmistakably possessing a power that is revealed when she is presented in close-up. This scene too seems oddly prescient, and one's sense of both the prescience and projection are produced

Figure 25. In his violent seduction of Anna, Stephen betrays family, friends, and self. (Courtesy Weintraub Entertainment Ltd.)

principally by Stephen-narrator, who interprets his memories. If Charley holds a position of control and ironic perspective *within* the scene (know ingly projecting his own immorality onto Stephen), Stephen-narrator's own ironic perspective enfolds and contains this. Thus, Charley's superior knowledge in the scene is temporary and ultimately illusory from the perspective of the mindscreen narrator, who knows his own failings as well as Charley's.

Charley's arrogance in Stephen-narrator's memory of this scene contributes to irony of another sort that becomes evident in the third-person narration of a scene near the end of the film. In the later scene Stephen and Charley confront each other in Anna's room, watching her pack her belongings to leave Oxford. The viewer understands Stephen's perspective – a mixture of guilt and satisfaction – because it has been revealed in Stephen-narrator's narration of time-past, in the omniscient narration within which the time-past narration has been embedded, and in the interaction of the two. Stephen refuses to tell the bewildered Charley anything about the accident that killed William, Anna's participation in it, or Stephen's own involvement in the subsequent events. The tables have turned, even if only Stephen and the omniscient narration (and viewer) know that. Not surprisingly, the scene in Anna's room is more likely to cause the viewer to recognize the significance of multiple levels of narration than those that make up time-past, simply because the narration of time-past is now past also. In the later scene the viewer possesses more knowledge and is aware of it, and the later knowledge sheds light on the earlier.

The interaction of the two levels of narration is especially telling in the reflexivity of Charley's storytelling enterprise. Whereas the extent to which Charley's story was a projection went unrecognized by Stephen-character, who came to possess that knowledge only later, it is known to Stephen-narrator, who temporarily suppresses it. Further, by its "acquiescence" in the suppression, the omniscient narration is implicated in the first-person narrator's strategy. In story terms the projection, and the sexual liaison between Charley and Anna on which it is partly based, occur well before they are revealed at both levels of the discourse. Moreover, the revelation that this is a story within a story perhaps belongs more to the omniscient narration than to the Stephen who is remembering the incident. Still another level of reflexivity belongs exclusively to the third-person narration, which reflects, as it were, on the power and possibilities (and limits) of stories to discover answers or provide proofs – a theme also articulated in Mosley's novel, whose narrator says, "It's true that art is the medium to provide answers, but these will of course be outside the scope of reason, which is all that can actually prove anything" (1967, 23–24). Just as Charley's story "knew" more than perhaps Charley himself did, so, too, Stephen-narrator's story knows more than its teller. And the omniscient narration knows, or reflexively comments on, stories, storytelling, and art itself.

The most problematic sequence in the film is Stephen's evening with Francesca (Delphine Seyrig) in which the narration's nonsynchronous image and sound tracks call attention to the telling rather than just the tale. In his petty competition with Charley, Stephen has arranged an appointment with a television producer in London for whom Charley is a regular performer. When the producer is absent because of a sudden illness, Stephen is put off by a glib subordinate (amusingly played by Pinter himself), who insinuatingly mentions the college provost's daughter, Francesca, with whom Stephen had an affair some years earlier. Seeking to shore up his already fragile self-confidence, and doubtless to compensate for his frustrated sexual obsession with Anna, Stephen impulsively telephones Francesca and takes her to dinner. Afterwards they return to her flat and have sex. The entire encounter is narrated in romanticized images that are at odds with intermittent, nonsynchronous dialogue the characters may or may not have actually said. In either case, the heard dialogue is obviously not the whole dialogue. The two characters are seen greeting one another, apparently reminiscing, having dinner, returning to her place, and finally lying in bed after their lovemaking.

At no time are they actually seen speaking, but at intervals during the sequence they are heard (in voice-over) uttering banal, conspicuously insincere sentiments about being happy and unchanged since the days of their more youthful affair.

Because its rendering is unlike anything else in the film, the Francesca sequence foregrounds questions about levels of narration. The expressive elements – including the retreating camera that draws back from scenes, often ending in a high-angle shot of long duration; the obsessive repetition of dialogue and the many unanswered questions the couple asks each other; and most extreme and disconcerting of all, the disjunction of image and sound – are so emphatic that commentary seems their primary purpose. And one may feel that commentary this overt is the province of the omniscient narration rather than Stephen's. This possibility, however, leads to the view that the character-narration has been preempted altogether, which is exceedingly unlikely unless one argues for a complete rupture in the text. A more persuasive argument takes account of the overall logic of the film's narration and the fact that Stephen's character-narration has involved self-judgment all along.

The disembodied voices and mute characters in the Francesca sequence convey Stephen's sense of simultaneous presence and absence. Viewed through the rain streaked window of a restaurant, the couple plays out a conventional liaison with a lassitude that underlines the lack of conviction in their persistent attempts to reassure each other of their ageless, ideal, unchanging selves. As a character in the sequence, Stephen is contradictory – weak, indecisive, opportunistic, sentimental. But the Stephen who narrates this tryst both reveals himself and deepens its irony when, for example, in the opening shot of the restaurant scene, he remembers a wall mural of a nude Adam and Eve (holding an apple). Although such a shot can be attributed to the omniscient narration whose perspective undercuts the characters' superficial intimacy, nothing requires that the viewer separate this narrational stance from Stephen's. As the narrator of time-past, Stephen offers an ironic, dissociated commentary on his own displaced desire. If this view is shared by the overall narration, the judgment is Stephen's nonetheless. Whatever a viewer might conclude about this slightly pathetic reunion, the character-narrator goes well beyond simply understanding it as a wistful charade. The narration is obviously figurative – characters whose mouths never open, enacting sentimental "brief encounter" roles, while their own disembodied voices punctuate and expose the falsehood. Overall, this most obvious and perhaps severest judgment of the mindscreen narration is revealingly centered on sexual sham, on an emotional dishonesty so basic as to be immoral.[6] Significantly, this corrupt idyll is succeeded by a still more corrupt act, for in the very next scene, Stephen-character plays panderer to his own competitor.

Returning to his supposedly empty home (Rosalind is spending the last days of her pregnancy at her mother's), Stephen is shocked to find Charley and Anna and realizes they are having an affair. His defeat as a player in this dark game would seem complete, but as the character-narration reveals, Stephen is a secret player in another, still darker game. Giving Charley a key to his house, Stephen becomes a vicarious and cowardly collaborator in Charley's sexual relationship with Anna. With cool self-possession, Stephen thus surrenders to his obsession and his darker self. The character-narrator has now foreshadowed, however unwittingly, the outcome of the long night during which he is actually telling his story. When the discourse returns to time-present and character-narration yields to the film's overall third-person narration, this darker self prevails as Stephen moves relentlessly to possess Anna sexually.

In the final scenes, the third-person omniscient narration assumes the viewer's now larger knowledge of Stephen's character and recounts the violent playing out of his moral tragedy. This is not, of course, the only tragedy. As Losey once said when referring to the accident that claims William's life, "It was a tragedy but not *the* tragedy. It was a catalyst, as the girl was a catalyst" (Milne 1968, 18–19). With the return to time-present, the third-person narration reveals how all other circumstances and considerations – including William's death (in story time only minutes ago) and the fact that Rosalind is about to give birth – are forced aside by the urgency of Stephen's sexual obsession (Figure 25). His behavior after the accident is at its coldest and most destructive, and yet, as Pinter said when speaking of the film overall, "the unforgivable, unforgettable things are never said" (Taylor 1966, 184). The third-person narration is almost disconcertingly oblique and elliptical, maintaining a firm distance from all but the first rush of Stephen's confrontation with Anna in the bedroom. This narrational stance confirms that the film's subject is not precisely events. Rather, the private moral implications of Stephen's actions, their place in his inner life, is the principal concern, and the narration signals one to look beyond events to the realm of Stephen's consciousness. For finally Stephen proves to be too weak a man to resist his desires and too honest to forget them. Significantly, this psychological insight and moral judgment are produced by neither third-person nor character-narration alone; they arise from their interaction.

The interaction of both levels of narration is nowhere more apparent or suggestive than in *Accident*'s final scene, which is almost a mirror image of the first scene. At the beginning of the film the third-person narration presents an exterior nighttime view of Stephen's house at the time of the car crash. In a silence broken at first only by the distant sound of a plane flying overhead, the camera remains absolutely still for several minutes (the opening credits are superimposed). As the off-screen sound of the accelerating car becomes audible, the camera begins a slow forward movement toward the facade of the house, stopping at the moment when the fatal crash is heard. By contrast, in the last scene the third-person narration, viewing Stephen's house in daylight, begins at the forwardmost point of the camera in the opening scene. Stephen's children are playing in the courtyard in front of the house when his daughter trips and falls. He emerges to rescue her and takes the children inside, closing the door behind him. Only then does the camera begin to withdraw, coming to rest outside the gate at the very place where the film begins (Figure 27). This concluding image, completing a circle whose path the narration has traced, establishes closure and may even suggest a restoration of the emotional and moral equilibrium that presumably marked Stephen's life before the story began. But the discourse presents more than an image. Throughout this last scene, the "natural" sounds are nearly drowned out by the repeated sound of the accident. Exactly as in the first scene, the sound grows louder and seems to come nearer until, just as the camera comes to rest, the crash itself is heard again – and then silence. The apparent restoration of Stephen's world, unchanged and untroubled, is, one now knows, an illusion. If he seems to have escaped the consequences of his actions, that is only a matter of seeming, of appearances. The accident and its aftermath, the combination of tragedies, betrayals, and violence, deny escape and belie the ordered surfaces and forms of Stephen's life.

The repeated sound of the car accident, then, is best understood as both the third-person narration's metaphor for Stephen's ongoing moral tragedy – an assertion of the inescapable presentness of his past – and also as subjective sound, what Stephen's mind figuratively hears and cannot evade. This interpretation is reinforced in the penultimate scene of the film, where a silent Stephen walks through the cloisters at Oxford (Figure 26). Over this continuous shot of him, the bells of the Oxford towers join with the sounds of the accelerating car, the rising noise level of the approaching car acting as a sound bridge to the final scene. Although both levels of narration are present in these last moments, one is inclined to privilege character-narration because of its importance and function in the narrative overall. The crucial issue is this: first-person narration enlarges the characterization

Figure 26. Over this shot of Stephen at Oxford, the sound of the car accident is heard once again, serving as the omniscient narration's reminder of the ongoing tragedy and the subjective sound of the accident replaying in Stephen's mind. (Courtesy Weintraub Entertainment Ltd.)

and modifies the meaning of the film as a whole by foregrounding Stephen's judgment of himself. Character and characterization are at the heart of *Accident* and depend on the interaction of these levels of narration. If time-past is not understood as character subjectivity, the theme of consciousness – perhaps one should call it self-consciousness – would be much diminished, if not altogether absent.

A more wide-ranging discussion of *Accident,* not focused precisely on the complexities of the film's narration, would touch on much that this chapter has thus far slighted and that must receive less attention here than we would like. Among the topics would be the character of Anna and her role in the story, Stephen's relationship with William, the motif of games, the character of the provost of Stephen's college, Oxford itself as a kind of character. Not all of these topics have equal weight, but all of them are important to the density of observation and insight that characterizes the film.

First-time viewers are frequently perplexed by Anna's character and role. She is, by any measure, an exceedingly enigmatic figure – quite apart from Jacqueline Sassard's narrow range as an actress, a failure much commented on by reviewers, and all the more noticeable for the wonderful performances

Figure 27. The repeated sound of the accident continues over the next (and final) scene as Stephen helps his daughter. The formal closure of *Accident* will end where the film began, with a placid view of Stephen's house. (Courtesy Weintraub Entertainment Ltd.)

that surround hers. In the novel, Mosley's Stephen remarks about Anna (whose physical description is quite different from Sassard): "We were fascinated because of that nothingness about her, so that we could put anything we liked onto her" (1967, 47). Nothing in Stephen-narrator's tale in the film suggests that he has this perception, but the novel's characterization of Anna is much the same as the film's nonetheless. (Some critics have seen her character as consistent with a negative view of women they find in Losey's films, not just those made with Pinter.) But Anna, in the film as in the novel, is not so much a character of understandable traits and motives as she is a figure on whom the various men – Stephen, Charley, and William – project what they want to see, even, one suspects, what they will "find" in one beautiful young woman if not the other. In this sense Anna is their creation – perhaps one should use the plural, for there are several Annas born of the men's different needs, desires, and self-conceptions (to say nothing of the viewer's response). To insist on defining her character more specifically would be to redefine the basic terms of the film, shifting attention from the (arrogant?) innocence of William, and the sometimes willful naïveté and folly of Charley and then Stephen, to the different matter of how their views tally with the reality of this object of their pursuit. And there can be no doubt that Anna is principally an object to them, rather than an individual. Why does Anna have an affair with Charley, whose attractions are mixed at best? Why does she decide to marry William? Why does she ask Stephen to tell Charley of her decision? How willing or knowing a seductress (or victim) is she when it comes to Stephen? All of these questions are left unanswered, because the uncertainty of Anna's motives and intentions, her own private self, is exactly what remains unknown and unknowable to the men and, along with her beauty, what fuels their fateful desires and competition.

When Anna is first glimpsed, in the earliest scene of the time-past narration, by William and Stephen from the window of Stephen's room at Oxford, she is a remote figure, beautiful and undefined, perhaps already a little mysterious. (Appropriately, Anna stops to pet a goat, a traditional symbol of lust, tethered on the lawn below Stephen's window.) In that moment, for all the easy intimacy and conviviality that obviously exist between the don and his aristocratic student, a foreign element appears – not exactly Anna herself, although her foreignness is implicitly a part of her allure, but the subtlest opening of a gulf between William and Stephen that the younger man fails to recognize at the time and probably never does. It is unclear just how aware Stephen is that he has already begun to compromise this friendship that he clearly values. The scene closes when Stephen offers to introduce the two young people and William declines. A kind of game has begun. William is, of course, both the victor and the victim in this game in which he does not even know he is a player. But his eventual death and its aftermath may obscure his place as an important person in Stephen's life. In a fashion more common to British universities than American, this youth and his tutor know each other rather well and share an appealing friendship that can easily be lost sight of in one's growing awareness of the unacknowledged passions that compel the adults into whose world William has happened.

If youth itself seems William's principal virtue, Stephen-narrator's memory recalls details, modest in their own right, that reveal William in more appealing terms than simply the unearned Edenic grace of a young man who has not yet been cast out of the garden. Oddly, though, some critics have perceived William as an arrogant, almost malicious competitor who consciously challenges Stephen with jibes about middle age or being sexually "past it," but such views ignore or misunderstand the tone of their scenes together. For example, when Stephen returns to his room in college immediately after his humiliating fall into the river while punting with William and Anna, William first teases him affectionately: "You look very dignified." "I feel wet," Stephen says. "Well, you don't look wet.... Nobody looked at you and said you were wet, did they? They thought you were quite normal." To Stephen's bitter complaint that he is growing old, William replies, "I wouldn't say you looked old. You've still got a pretty good figure." Admittedly a young man's reassurance can salt the wound it is meant to heal, but William's remarks do not belong to a youth without feeling or consideration. Quite the contrary. "It's nice knowing you," he says quietly to Stephen a few minutes later when the two of them sit together on a couch sharing a bottle of scotch. "You're not a bad fellow for a philosophy tutor." Their conversation concludes with the exchange about aristocrats being meant to be killed. The irony of William's reply – "Of course. They're immortal" – inevitably dominates one's sense of the scene, but the conversation has revealed neither tension nor insensitivity on William's part. Indeed, for Stephen-narrator, the remembered scene is no less poignant than ironic.

Stephen's friendship with William does not, however, prevent him from deliberately making moves (with William and others) intended to secure an advantage with Anna that he never openly admits until their final, solitary time together. From one point of view, Stephen moves and countermoves in a seemingly endless series of games in which all the characters are players, whether they always know it or not. The deadliest games, of course, are those that are never acknowledged, but the film is marked as well by games of a more formal sort: tennis during the Sunday sequence, a cricket match on the day of William's death, during which his youth bests Charley's now aging prowess, and a ferocious contest (based on the so-called Eton wall game) at William's ancestral country home when he insists that Stephen play goal. This is the only scene in which competition between William and Stephen is overt; similarly, William's insistence that Stephen play ("Only the old men watch, and the ladies") is the only time that an aristocratic arrogance on his part seems apparent. *Accident* is full of games and "games," metaphors for the kinds of lethal competitions whose outcome none of the players is quite prepared for.

In the film's last formal game, the cricket match played in the afternoon of the day of William's death, Stephen stands on the sidelines, behind the provost of his college, while William leads his team to victory over Charley's. The contest between Anna's lover, Charley, and her yet undisclosed fiancé, William, is evident at both narrational levels, but it is not the cruelest game being played. Admiring William as a "magnificent young athlete," the provost (Alexander Knox), whose gloved malice has been hinted at before, asks

Stephen if he was good at games when he was young. To Stephen's admission that he was not, the provost replies only with a private and slyly knowing smile. In the immediate terms of the narrative the provost's reaction is irrelevant, but it nonetheless exposes him as just as heartless a player in the game of power as any of the others. When Stephen tells the provost that he has recently seen his daughter, Francesca, the provost pretends not even to know whom Stephen is referring to. Finally he says to Stephen, with cool calculation, "Ah, give her my love." In its own way, this moment is one of the most chilling in the film.

Despite the film's considerable originality, and making allowances for its unusually measured tempo and stylistic departures, such as the Francesca sequence, *Accident* has been seen by some reviewers as simply an instance (although admittedly an eccentric one) of classical film narration. The transitions into and out of time-past, for example, have been treated as little more than sophisticated variations on the optical and aural cues with which flashbacks have traditionally been introduced and concluded. But to conceive the film in these terms is to oversimplify to the point of reductiveness not only *Accident* but the artistic resources of the medium. One need not have thought about the possible complexities of filmic narration to recognize that Losey and Pinter have more in mind than an indictment of middle-aged infidelity and guilt. Instead, the film's experiment with narrational voices and point of view in the mode of art cinema is concerned not simply with action or plot, but with the expression of individual consciousness – not just with events but with the reverberation of events in the inner life. "No physical violence," Losey said, "only the inner violence of what people feel" (Milne 1968, 19). Certainly *Accident* does not pretend to offer a model of how the mind works, nor have narrative films, including art cinema, generally sought to do so. *Accident* belongs to that relatively small body of works that have expanded one's understanding of the uncertainties and hidden recesses of human experience by invoking the resources of film art rather than science or psychology or even reason. Everything happens; nothing is explained; the presentness of the past; the need to both forget and remember – these are the film's themes, its answers, to invoke the notion expressed by the novel's narrator. *Accident* is neither the first nor the last of Losey's films to concern itself with such matters, but in its subtle exploration of subjectivity in narration and characterization, it is the first to take so large a step artistically in confronting them.

In an interview given after both *Accident* and *The Go-Between* were completed, Harold Pinter commented: "I certainly feel more and more that the past is not past, that it never was past. It's present" (Gussow 1972, 25–6). The view is Losey's too, of course, and it has haunted much of his work, including such otherwise different films as *The Boy with Green Hair, Time Without Pity, Blind Date, The Criminal, Accident,* and *The Go-Between,* his next and last film with Pinter. Significantly, the last two films of the Losey–Pinter collaboration discover in the interaction of third-person narration and character-narration the discreteness of both time-present and time-past while making real their indivisibility. In *Accident* Stephen's emotional and moral dishonesty and his violent seduction of Anna betray the claims of both marriage and friendship, the claims of his own best self. The film's subtle modulation between third-person narration and character-narration reveals that although these betrayals occurred in the past, there is neither refuge nor relief in this fact. The past is indeed ever present, and it necessarily becomes the province of first-person narration when it enters the discourse as memory, a present, personal, and narrated-to-the-self event. The insight lies at the center of *Accident,* and it will be extended to an informing principle in *The Go-Between* with its complex narrational structure and double articulation of time.

5

"The Annihilation of Time"

The Go-Between

In 1971 at the Cannes festival the grand prize, the Palme d'or, was awarded to *The Go-Between,* Losey's last-produced film with Harold Pinter. Alexander Walker rightly called the film, which is based on a novel by L. P. Hartley, a "masterpiece," but like that of so many of Losey's films before and after it, the path of *The Go-Between* from inception to completion was tortuous. In this instance, however, delay proved fortunate. "Immediately after *The Servant* I took *The Go-Between* to Harold," Losey told Michel Ciment:

> He wrote a screenplay of about fifty or sixty pages. In the middle of his work the project broke up because a man got a hold of some subsidiary rights that blocked us. It was not revived until seven years later. And when we went back to that script, we found that we were not at all satisfied with it, which was a development simply of *The Servant* collaboration. (1985, 239)

The more adventurous collaboration on *Accident* had intervened, and Losey and Pinter had become, in Losey's words, "fascinated by the concept of time, and by the power the cinema has suddenly to reveal the meaning of a whole life" (304). Pinter told John Russell Taylor when *The Go-Between* was in production:

> Looking back at what I had done the first time, I realised that I had missed a whole aspect, perhaps to me now the most important aspect, of the book. I had concentrated on a straight dramatisation of the central story about the young boy and the lovers. Now what I find most exciting about the subject is the role of time: the annihilation of time by the man's return to the scene of his childhood experience. (1970, 203)

Shaped by Losey and Pinter's growing interest in film and time, and the increasing richness of their collaboration, *The Go-Between* is a remarkably complex and moving film.

The conception of time that fascinated Losey and Pinter and that informs *The Go-Between* is related to the philosophy of Henri Bergson, who was a major influence on Marcel Proust and Alain Resnais. In Bergson's view linear or clock time is produced by the analytical function of the intellect, which spatializes time, dividing it into one-directional discrete units, thus fragmenting the emotional life by separating past, present, and future. The result is a rupture in what should be whole. By contrast, pure time, as Bergson conceives it, is multidimensional; past, present, and future are fused.[1] (Given the relevance of Bergson's ideas, *The Go-Between* clearly presages Losey and Pinter's efforts to make a film based on *A la recherche du temps perdu*, Proust's classic meditation on time, memory, and meaning. So, too, the film has some similarities to Resnais's *Hiroshima mon amour* and *La guerre est finie* for the same reasons.) The "annihilation" of linear time proves not only a major theme in *The Go-Between*, but the key to its structure: a double articulation in the form of discrete but interacting narrations of present and past in the life of its central character.

The story events of the past, which constitute the majority of the discourse and are narrated chronologically, center on a middle-class English boy, Leo Colston (Dominic Guard). Spending a holiday at the lavish country home of a schoolmate during a scorchingly hot summer, young Leo, who was almost thirteen, was drawn unwittingly into being a messenger, a go-between, for the aristocratic Marian Maudsley (Julie Christie), the beautiful older sister of his friend, and Ted Burgess (Alan Bates), a handsome tenant farmer with whom she was having a secret affair. Anxious to please Marian – and only dimly aware of the implications of her relationship with Ted – Leo found himself trapped on a battleground of class conflict and adult sexuality. Suspecting the affair, Marian's mother, Mrs. Maudsley (Margaret Leighton), finally shed the mask of calm elegance that had hidden her suspicions and fears, dragging Leo from his birthday celebration and forcing him to go with her into the rain to discover the lovers having sex in their trysting place. This cruelly abrupt and shocking confrontation with adult sexuality and betrayal destroyed Leo emotionally, condemning him to an existence barren of love.

In Hartley's novel, which is narrated entirely in first-person, time-past is the main body of the discourse; the present is a framing story (including an epilogue) in which Leo Colston tells of finding the diary of his long-ago summer and his subsequent return to its sites. Time-past is thus mediated by the narrator, now an older man who, under the stimulus of the diary, concentrates on what he experienced as a youth. The impingement of the past on the present and the process of memory itself are revealed by the rendering of the past through the reflective and ironic sensibility of the mature narrator looking back on his life. His summary judgments of his youthful experience occur primarily in the framing story. The narrator remembers, for example, when, early in his visit, Marian took him to Norwich to buy a new (and cooler) summer wardrobe. After the shopping, Marian left him to amuse himself visiting the cathedral because, she said, she had some shopping of her own to do. Of the conclusion of that adventure, the narrator says:

> I hung around the statue, wondering who Sir Thomas Browne was, shy of getting into the carriage and sitting there as if I owned it; and then I caught sight of her on the far side of the square. She seemed to be saying goodbye to someone, at least I had the impression of a raised hat. She came slowly towards me, threading her way through the traffic, and did not see me till much later. Then she waved her parasol with its frilly, foamy edges and quickened her step. (1984, 49)

Marian was actually having a rendezvous with Ted, but the boy was absorbed in his own experience, which the adult remembers as a moment when he felt "it was glorious to be me, intimately satisfying to look like me" (48). In the epilogue the subjectivity of the narration acquires an additional aspect, for reflection and evaluation are added to simple recollection:

> I saw now, what I did not take in then, that her chief object in going to Norwich was to meet Ted Burgess: his must have been the raised hat on the other side of the square. But it would be unduly cynical to say I was only a pretext for her journey. It would have been an expensive pretext, for one thing – not that she minded about money. I felt pretty sure that she was genuinely concerned about my permanently overheated state and wanted to do me a good turn. Inexplicable as it seemed to me now, the conviction that she had never really cared for me had been the bitterest of the pills I had to swallow. (294–5)

The layering of time is evident in this passage, for in his memory the narrator joins his original experience to his later disillusionment upon realizing his betrayal, and enfolds both within his perspective some fifty years later. Only in the journey that is the narration itself does Leo Colston's experience as both child and adult acquire meaning. Narration, then, is an act of discovery for Hartley's Leo. And this is what attracted Losey and Pinter when they returned to the novel and compelled them to dismiss a simple presentation of the story of the young boy and the lovers.

In *Making Pictures: The Pinter Screenplays,* a study of Pinter's adaptations of novels rather than of his own stage plays, Joanne Klein argues that the writer habitually regards the past as "alive, but not real, the past exists as a property of the imagination, as a fictive rather than factual phenomenon" (1985, 801). But consider Pinter's remark quoted in the previous chapter: "I certainly feel more and more that the past is not past, that it never was past. It's present" (Gussow 1972, 25–6). This remark, uttered after both *Accident* and *The Go-Between* were completed, argues for the "realness" of the past as something more than mere recollections or even imagination. Neither Pinter nor Losey would accept the notion that the past is only fictive. "The past *is* rather than was," as Klein asserts, but the very heart of Losey and Pinter's view in *The Go-Between* is that the past is present as reality, not simply imaginative recollection. The notion of annihilating time necessarily leads to destroying the distinction between "is" and "was." In *The Go-Between* time only "is."

Working again within the broad outlines of art-cinema narration, Losey and Pinter extend the experiment in subjectivity begun in *Accident*. To annihilate time they reject its most potent manifestation in narrative generally – that is, a structure based on linear time, such as typically underlies classical narration and provides the fundamental basis for determining causality. As Robert Scholes has pointed out, *post hoc ergo propter hoc* (after the fact, therefore because of the fact), which is a fallacy in logic, "is a principle of fiction: that a cause and effect relationship links the temporal elements in any narrative sequence" (1979, 423).[2] (The most common variation on this principle is a simple flashback, conventionally framed by an activity such as dreaming or perhaps courtroom testimony that is understood to be its origin.) Rather than linear narration, then, in its double articulation of time the film provides parallel, interacting narrations. Moreover, voice-overs from the present in the past and the past in the present, and the nonchronological narration of the present, further militate against perceiving time in simple linear terms, or supposing a revelation of causality in Leo Colston's life to be the principal intention of the film. Instead, the subjectivizing of the interactive narrations is precisely about revealing a wholeness in which past and present exist as a single, indivisible reality. In this subtle, exceedingly complex structure, "threads which started off parallel gradually intertwine," as Losey said, "and in the end past and present are one and the same" (Ciment 1985, 304).

The narration of time-past is well under way in the film before one realizes that the occasional intervention of brief scenes in time-present of a conservatively dressed older man, shown in the rain at various sites that were part of young Leo's experience, narrate the return of the elderly Leo (Michael Redgrave) to the now changed landscape of his boyhood summer. Although the discourse continues to suppress information that would readily establish the relationship of time-past and time-present, one eventually realizes their connection and the implication that the lively young Leo's experience at the turn of the century produced the somber, lifeless man who inhabits the gray and dismal present. Past and present, then, penetrate one another so that the boy's innocence and promise of life stand side by side with the man's death-in-life. Thus, the drama and poignance of *The Go-Between* are not merely that of the boy's lost innocence but of the man's desolation as well. Even when one realizes that young Leo's experience produced the elder Leo's bleakness, however, there remain questions about how to interpret the narration.

At the first level the film presents an omniscient narration of time-present, which tells the story of the older Leo Colston's return to the sites of his thirteenth summer; at the second level, the adult Leo narrates his memories of that summer. But there are ambiguities in the narration at both levels, most obviously in the voice-overs from both time periods and the nonchronological structure of the present. One's inclination is to explain discrepancies in both narrations (as distinct from the narratives they produce) in terms of characterization. The voice-overs, for instance, can often be accounted for either as the adult Leo's memories or as subjective judgments expressed in his character-narration of the past. The irregularity of the narration of time-present, however, is most unusual, for the omniscient narration permanently suppresses cues that would establish its full chronology. Moreover, the nonchronological structure subverts the implied claim of "objectivity" typical of omniscient narration. How, then, is one to interpret the subjectivized third-person narration of the present? Is it, too, an element of characterization, and if so, in what sense? The answer to these questions is not immediately apparent; there is, in fact, no single moment when it is revealed. But gradually it becomes clear that the atemporality of the time-present narration expresses the subjective experience of the older Leo, the emotional incoherence or discontinuity that has excluded him from the fullness of life ever since his fateful encounter a half-century ago.

The film's opening shot behind the credits is deceptively simple. In close-up the camera slowly tilts down a rain-spattered windowpane through which, at first, nothing can be seen. As the raindrops slip down the surface of the glass, indistinct shapes, a blurred landscape, appear barely visible beyond (Figure 28). Accompanied by the descending chords of the musical score, this downward movement (of raindrops and camera) comes to an end as the camera moves toward the glass and seems to pass through it into a brilliantly sunny long shot of an English manor house. As the long shot holds, a man's voice-over states: "The past is a foreign country. They do things differently there." An evocative opening, to be sure, not least for the questions it raises about the juxtaposition of the rainy windowpane and sun-drenched landscape and the relationship between the voice-over and the image. Only as the film progresses does one retrospectively come to understand that the Leo Colston of the present has spoken, but the first bright warm view of Brandham Hall and the following shot of two young boys riding in a carriage through the beautiful Norfolk countryside introduce the Leo Colston of the past. Thus, the film's double articulation of time is operative from the beginning in the intersection of the subjectivized omniscience of time-present and the older Leo's character-narration or mindscreen of the past. Importantly, *The Go-Between* begins, however briefly, in the present, only to move into a sustained time-past sequence where young Leo is introduced to Brandham Hall and the Maudsley family. (A small but crucial difference between this opening and that of Pinter's published screenplay is that the screenplay begins not with the time-present image of the rainy glass, but with a time-past shot of the sunny English countryside.) In Losey's complicated enunciation of narrational levels, the time-present image is followed by an image from time-past over which is heard the time-present voice of the adult Leo. The initial disjuncture between sound and image will be repeated with variations throughout both levels of the narration and will become a defining trait of the discourse's interrogation of time.

From the beginning Losey's fascination with houses that are revelatory of the characters and conflicts they enclose is fully exploited in the story of Leo, both boy and man, who becomes first entranced and then entrapped by the Maudsley mansion. The opening scenes of Leo's introduction to the Maudsley household capture, through the extended motif of windows, stairs, and doors, both the awe and enthrallment of the boy and the irony

95

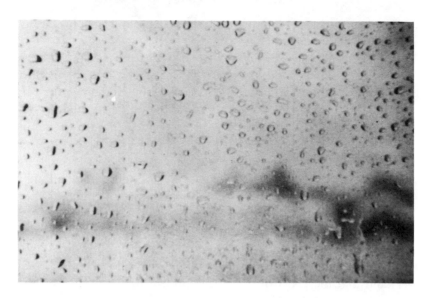

Figure 28. *The Go-Between* begins with the time-present image of the rain-spattered windowpane that comes to be associated with the older Leo. This image gives way to the sun-drenched world of young Leo and time-past. (Courtesy Weintraub Entertainment Ltd.)

of the omniscient narration's perspective. These windows, stairs, and doors are all passageways, the means whereby one may look into or enter another place. The several and varied passageways of the film include more obviously the doors into the Hall or from room to room, the intricate stairways that both separate and link distinct social worlds, and the windows through which young Leo first observes the Hall's beautiful inhabitants – particularly Marian. Thus, the film's first sequence (including the titles) introduces not only most of the principal characters, but the carefully elaborated formal design that governs the narration as a whole.

As Leo enters Brandham Hall, the camera follows him through a doorway and up the winding stairs to his friend Marcus's room. Shown at first through a window as he begins to climb the stairs, Leo stops on a landing to look through another window at the distant figures of Marian and the Maudsleys' houseguests on the lawn below. Once in the room he goes to a window to look at them again. Leaving the room, Leo and Marcus go downstairs, their progress marked by a series of shots through still more windows, each of which shows the languid, elegant figures more closely. Although it seems a simple use of the motif at this point in the film, symbolizing Leo's entrance into a new world and his curiosity about the beautiful but remote people

Figure 29. On Brandham Hall's great central staircase, young Leo is surrounded by imposing portraits when he is surprised by Marcus emerging from a secret hiding place. (Courtesy Weintraub Entertainment Ltd.)

Figure 30. "Immortals, inheritors of the summer," the novel's narrator calls Ted and Hugh, an attitude expressed in this low-angle shot showing young Leo with his competing heroes just before they do battle in the cricket match. (Courtesy Weintraub Entertainment Ltd.)

who belong there, the simplicity is more apparent than real, for the narration has already linked implicitly the rainy windowpane to the clear windows through which young Leo first sees this golden world beckoning to him. The boys' descent down the stairs also includes a brief incident that seems a paradigm for Leo's experience. Marcus, who has run down the stairs ahead of Leo, opens and then hides behind a secret door off one of the landings. When Leo stops on the landing and looks up at the large, imposing portraits lining the stairway, Marcus suddenly jumps out from his hiding place to grab him from behind, and the two begin to scuffle (Figure 29). Such child's play portends something more, for the older Leo knows what the young Leo will learn at great cost – what seems grand, stately, and elegant about the aristocracy can be a veil for what is labyrinthine, secretive, dangerous, and destructive.

Once Leo has moved outside the Hall, joining the world beyond the doorways and windows that he has been looking through, he skirts by Marian, dressed in white and lying in a hammock. He seems perhaps already to have fallen under her spell, the first slight instance of another motif, that of spells and curses, that will play a major role in the film. As he continues to explore the grounds of the estate with Marcus, Leo must slip by the "deadly nightshade" plant (*Atropa belladonna,* he correctly identifies it) in the old garden. Leo's contact with the poisonous belladonna (beautiful lady) as he brushes against it is a visual metaphor foreshadowing the final consequences of his relationship with Marian. From the omniscient narration's perspective on the fate of the adult Leo, these scenes are most ironic, for young Leo is famous at school as a magician, a sorcerer who has made two classmates fall off a roof. At the first dinner with the family, the boy explains why his victims did not perish: "Well, it wasn't a killing curse, you see. There are curses and curses. It depends on the curse." Leo's innocence stands in dark contrast to the fact that he will learn too much too soon about killing curses. Only later can one appreciate the full irony in Marian's question to him during that first dinner: "You're not going to bewitch us here, are you?"

A good deal of the film's symbolism – colors, sorcery, the zodiac, the sun – arises from Hartley's novel. Losey often extends these by purely visual means, particularly in the case of colors and the sun, the latter associated specifically with Marian. Moreover, in both the film and the novel the various patterns of symbols are densely interwoven, so that an element of one pattern becomes an element of another as well, weaving together even more tightly the separate threads of the narration. Frequently, the film's dialogue and visual imagery center on Leo's interest in sorcery. The middle-class boy has entered the godlike world of the upper classes. (The novel's narrator says, "In my eyes the actors in my drama had been immortals, inheritors of the summer" [1984, 293].) The signs of the zodiac cover the front page of the diary where he keeps a detailed record of his spells, and he associates himself with the dominating Leo of the zodiac, who is ruled only by the sun. As he takes on his role as the go-between, first carrying messages for Marian's fiancé, Hugh Trimingham (Edward Fox), and then for the farmer, Ted Burgess, Leo begins to lose his identity. Hugh calls him Mercury, the messenger of the gods, although Leo, interestingly, knows Mercury only as the smallest of the planets and the one nearest the sun. For Ted, Leo is simply the "postman," but one who will eventually "catch out" Ted in both the cricket match and the dangerous game of love (Figure 30). Marian supplies Leo with new clothes and a new identity that entangles him in an aristocratic world and sexual intrigue as fascinating as it is mystifying to him. When early in the film young Leo turns to a spell in an effort to check the mounting heat, he is unsuccessful; the next day the temperature has climbed another degree. He and Marian's father mark each day's rising temperature that foreshadows the approach of the traumatic climax that must inevitably end the summer. The summer heat that permeates the world at the Hall parallels the passionate affair of Ted and Marian, as well as Leo's own awakening sexuality.

When Leo arrives at the Hall wearing a brown Norfolk coat whose style and color match the formal lines and rich brown tones of the Hall, he is conspicuously the outsider, the object of family joking because his heavy wool coat is out of keeping with the hot summer weather. The new suit of clothes that Marian buys him on their expedition to Norwich is Lincoln green, and later she intends to give him a green bicycle for his birthday. Leo is closely associated with green – it's "your true color," Marcus tells him, "Marian said so" – not only because of his inexperience and envy of the aristocratic world, but also because he plays a kind of Robin Hood to her Maid Marian, who consciously courts his attentions and uses his adolescent infatuation for her own devious purposes. And this Robin Hood helps steal, however unwittingly, the aristocratic Marian for Ted Burgess, the tenant of Black Farm. Red, too, is associated with Leo, who cuts his leg sliding down Ted's haystack and who later becomes upset at the sight of rabbit's blood that Ted, returning from hunting, smears on one of Marian's letters. This bloodletting foreshadows the violent end to the affair and Ted's suicide. At the height of his glory, Leo is called on to sing a song to the assembly of aristocrats and farmers after he has caught out Ted in the annual cricket match. The song, which is in fact a hymn, nicely describes

Figure 31. Accompanying the time-present view of the older Leo at the cemetery is young Leo's voice-over: "Well, it wasn't a killing curse, you see. It depends on the curse." (Courtesy Weintraub Entertainment Ltd.)

his attitude toward and relationship with Marian, for he sings: "Angels! Ever bright and fair, / Take, oh take me to your care. / Speed to your own courts my flight / Clad in robes of virgin white." Moreover, as he sings, Leo stands in front of the Union Jack, whose red stripes, as they are framed in the image, form a large cross behind him, making him, visually at least, a victim even in his moment of triumph (see Figure 34). The import of the latter image cannot, of course, have been apparent to the boy, but to the elder Leo who is narrating time-past, the irony is not only deeply embedded in his memory but all too clear.

A more complex instance in the narration's dual threads fuses symbolism and irony with the discourse's characteristic layering of perspectives to brilliant and suggestive effect. During their carriage ride to Norwich to shop for Leo's new clothes, the older Leo remembers, Marian sat opposite him with her parasol open so that it was luminous and sunlit, as if all the golden light belonged to her. At this moment, one hears the second voice-over, in which the adult Leo says, "You flew too near the sun and you were scorched" (Figure 32). Sound and image join here to show the boy's physical point of view while the voice-over from the present, speaking, significantly, in the

Figure 32. Marian is seen from young Leo's point of view, while the adult Leo's voice-over pronounces a judgment: "You flew too near the sun and you were scorched." (Courtesy Weintraub Entertainment Ltd.)

Figure 33. The image with its "rooms within rooms" in the Maudsley house suggests the labyrinthine intrigue that entraps Leo in his role as Marian's go-between. (Courtesy Weintraub Entertainment Ltd.)

second person, iterates the older man's sense of his younger self as a totally different character and, poignantly if not tragically, his judgment on that earlier self as guilty of a kind of hubris. For the man, responsibility belongs to the boy rather than the adults who used him so carelessly. When he sits across from Marian with her golden parasol or, in a later scene, next to the large brass horn of the gramophone in the smoking room, one is visually reminded of Leo's flight too near the sun.

In its rendering of these scenes from the past and of the adult Leo in whose mind they dwell, *The Go-Between* is about both memories and the process of memory itself. For, as Henri Bergson believed, memory is not mere preservation; memory creates. The unfolding vision of that long-ago summer, then, is not presented simply as a record; the images are simultaneously Leo's memories and the visual equivalent of memory's journey into the past. A deceptively simple use of camera and sound suggests this complex dimension of the film. For example, Marian, Ted, and Hugh are all seen at some length before they first speak, a pattern that may suggest the particularly insistent quality of visual recollection. Indeed, young Leo himself sees the surrounding countryside, the house, and Marcus's bedroom before either he or Marcus speaks a word. It is as if in the mind of the adult Leo the past can be seen before it is heard. The handling of time in the film is like a palimpsest, a layering of different times and perspectives within any given moment, whereas in the novel the older Leo's perspective is most overt in the prologue and epilogue. It is in the epilogue, for instance, that the adult Leo comments on his reluctance to think about what happened to those "others" who experienced that summer with him and survived. Leo comments:

> As to these "others" of Brandham Hall, somehow I could not think of them as going on after I had stopped. They were like figures in a picture, the frame enclosed them, the twofold frame of time and place, and they could not step outside it, they were imprisoned in Brandham Hall and the summer of 1900. There let them stay, fixed in their two dimensions: I did not want to free them. (Hartley 1984, 296)

This simile is put to a different use in the film by helping to convey the process as well as the substance of memory. The figures of the past – particularly when Leo sees them through the windows and at the moment before the dinner when he first sees all the Maudsleys together – are often grouped into tableaux, like formal portraits from an album of memories. Losey is subtle rather than emphatic in his use of such moments, but they nonetheless emphasize this quality of Leo's memory. Similarly, those moments when the camera holds on the landscape, or the instance when the camera holds for several seconds on a Norwich street from which young Leo and Marian have just disappeared around a corner, convey a kind of contemplation and attention that is itself an action.

Memory as both fact and act is foregrounded in several ways that are specifically cinematic. Consider, for example, the scene in Norwich when Leo first sees Marian and Ted together. After leaving the cathedral, Leo walks into the city's square. In a shot that begins with the boy entering the left foreground and Ted and Marian across the square in the right background, the camera then dollies forward past Leo. Initially the shot frames the youthful figure of Leo's remembered self. As the camera moves forward, though, excluding him from the frame, it in effect combines one form of subjective vision – memory in its simplest terms – with another that corresponds closely (but not exactly) to the physical point of view of young Leo as he watches the figures across the square. The movement of the camera is a purely cinematic metaphor for the movement of the adult Leo's mind, his act of concentration as he enters more deeply and fully into the past. One cannot argue that the adult Leo's narration here conveys anything like the details of judgment and sense of betrayal that the passage from the novel's epilogue contains; however, in Losey's sophisticated command of point of view, the subjective realm of time-past is not fixed but dynamic, alive in its power to compel Leo's attention. Further, the discourse's first intercut to a time-present scene, a shot of the older Leo at the church cemetery, appears in the midst of the sequence just as the boy leaves the cathedral immediately before he sees Marian and Ted. Even without an explanation of their relationship, the intercutting of these scenes necessarily affects one's response to the character-narration, for the potential unity of a past moment filled with youthful innocence and curiosity is invaded by the silence and solemnity of the present. This proves to be a deeply suggestive pattern in the film, for its interacting narrations reveal a Leo whse life has, in a sense, been inverted. For Leo, ironically, it is the past that is prey to the present, not the reverse. What the prologue and epilogue accomplish in the novel thus becomes an ongoing, elucidating process from first image to last in the film.

After the first two voice-overs – "The past is a foreign country" and "You flew too near the sun" – the discourse intermittently presents brief scenes of the older Leo in time-present returning to the sites of his past. This, even more than the voice-overs, is what begins to radicalize the narration. The first of these scenes (actually the second time-present image, the first being the rainy window behind the credits) shows from the back a man staring through the gates of a church cemetery. The motionless, forlorn figure, wearing a gray raincoat and bowler and carrying an umbrella, appears only to be a staid, almost too conventionally attired gentleman whose temporal and physical location are unexplainable. Not until later does one realize that the aging Leo is visiting the graves of those who peopled his remembered world (Figure 31). That summer, one eventually learns, also marked his own psychological and emotional death, but this insight is virtually inaccessible at this early stage in the narration. Further, not only is the time-present moment unexplainable for lack of cues provided by the discourse, but its intrusiveness is compounded by an accompanying voice-over. Over the image from the present the now familiar voice of young Leo is heard repeating the lines one heard him say at his first dinner at the Hall: "Well, it wasn't a killing curse, you see. There are curses and curses. It depends on the curse." Irony is obvious in the juxtaposition of a youth's pronouncement about "killing curses" to the image of a graveyard, but beyond this one is at a loss to interpret the scene fully. Nonetheless, a substantial number of the elements that inform the third-person narration have been introduced and foregrounded; many of their details, however, remain suspended. Their import will emerge only little by little with great complexity in subsequent scenes.

When the discourse presents the second and third time-present scenes – a fragment of Leo's arrival at the Norwich train station and his arrival outside the church where he visits the graveyard – one realizes that the first three time-present scenes (excluding the film's initial image) are not narrated chronologically. They appear, instead, in a 3–1–2 order: Leo standing at the churchyard cemetery, then turning and walking away; next stepping into a car after arriving at the Norwich station; and then the car drawing up to the church. The fourth time-present scene shows Leo in the foreground of an over-the-shoulder long shot of a house one later learns is lived in by the now aged Lady Trimingham, who, as the beautiful Marian Maudsley, was the reckless enchantress of Leo's boyhood. As impossible to locate precisely as the others, the fourth time-present scene nonetheless seems likely to occur later in story time than its predecessors. Once introduced, these time-present scenes appear with increasing if irregular frequency. Despite a persisting uncertainty as to their origin and their relationship to the coherent narration of time-past into which they intervene, these four scenes have some noticeable common elements. A dismal rainy day (apparently the same day), the recurring figure of the anonymous older man, and the impression that the sites are near one another – all suggest connections. Whatever their unknown relationships, and despite their separation in the narration of time-present, these scenes invite one to begin constructing another story than the one told by the character-narration of time-past.

With the conclusion of the fourth time-present scene, most of the features of the omniscient narration and its potential relationships to the character-narration of the past have been established. Particular sites recur in both time frames, inhabited by both versions of Leo. Dialogue from both periods is heard over images from the other. And there are suggestive associations between the present moments and the time-past scenes that immediately frame them. The adult's arrival in Norwich, for example, appears just when the boy, on his shopping expedition with Marian, is asked to amuse himself in the Norwich cathedral. Similarly, the car arrives at the cemetery immediately after Leo first compromises himself by supporting Marian's lie to her mother that they saw no one in the city. And the time-present long shot of the unidentified house in the village is preceded by the scene of the youth's entering the church with the family and followed by the congregation leaving the church, at which time young Leo first talks to Hugh Trimingham and carries his first, quite innocent message: Marian has forgotten her prayer book. Further, although one knows nothing yet of the house or its present occupant, it has already appeared in time-past.

Interestingly, while the time-present scenes are not flash-forwards, they have sometimes been regarded as such. The key to understanding this phenomenon lies in a detail that has already been emphasized: the film's first image is in the present. Leo Colston's past had a unity shattered by the passions of a self-centered aristocratic world indifferent to the boy. Consequently, the emotional integrity of his past, manifest in the chronological structure and golden tones of his character-narration, can seem to trigger the discontinuous, apparently random immediacy of a present whose only meaning resides in memories the man can neither escape nor make his own. The adult Leo's present is not just "dried up," as Marian later says; it is without the simplest form of connectedness. When contrasted with the mindscreen's unity, the fragmentation and confusing lack of sequence of the third-person narration express the subjective reality of a man for whom the present is an uncharted land – although, ironically, it is the past he declares a "foreign country." There seems an unbridgeable gulf between past and present Leo Colstons, an estrangement that defines his tragedy. Seeking to unify the two time periods in a single story, one also seeks to reconcile the two Leos. Ironically, this proves to be the very reason for Leo's return to this now alien landscape, even if he does not know it.

Once again Marian will ask Leo to be a go-between, this time to carry a message to her grandson, who is descended from her union with Ted Burgess, not Hugh Trimingham, the man she actually married. Marian wants Leo to assure the grandson that his lineage is no curse, that he is "the child of so much happiness and beauty." With her aristocratic illusions still intact, Marian is oblivious to her role in making the man, as she says, "all dried up inside." The scene in which Marian, now an old woman with only memories of her own, asks Leo to carry one last message is the climax of the omniscient narration of the present, and indeed of the larger realm of the entire film. The adult Leo cannot have known when he answered Marian's summons to return to the sites of his fateful summer holiday that its traumatic events and emotions have survived unresolved all these years. What can he have supposed Marian would now be like? And why would she turn to him again when the past, it would seem, is now quite dead and forgotten? The answers to these questions dominate the narration of the last long, exceedingly complex time-present sequence, which concludes the film. The character-narration of the past, however, has begun to provide answers, or at least the basis for them, even before the questions themselves can be defined.

In his youthful and eager desire to please Marian, young Leo willingly if innocently conspires with her. In what was initially an alliance that fed his half-formed infatuation, Leo finds himself Marian's increasingly confused and troubled "cavalier," which is Hugh's term for him. The messenger of the gods, their go-between, becomes a conspirator. His divided feelings of devotion and doubt are poignantly obvious in the character-narration when Hugh enters a room just as Marian is giving Leo another letter for Ted. Instinctively concealing the letter, he realizes at some level that this is a betrayal of Hugh, whose kindness and interest have also won his loyalty. As Hugh and Marian leave the room, Leo stands in the doorway while the camera pulls back until he is shown framed by a series of doorways (Figure 33). The image is a metaphor for Leo's dilemma, expressing his intuitive recognition that the adult world into which he has been drawn has rooms within rooms, levels of complexity and emotion that lie beyond his limited experience and understanding. Clutching Marian's letter, left unsealed in her haste, Leo is perplexed and unsettled, no longer the happy postman, as Ted has called him and as the elderly Marian will again before the film's conclusion. Finally, as he walks to Ted's farm, driven by his need to penetrate what has grown increasingly a mystery to him, Leo opens the letter. Seeing only the opening line – Marian's passionate "Darling, Darling, Darling" – he sinks to the base of a tree, his tears a painful indication of this disturbing discovery. If one is left uncertain how fully the adult Leo as mindscreen narrator understands all the implications of this event, the more ironic perspective of the overall third-person narration clearly embraces the memories as well as the man to whom they belong, implicitly commenting on the contradictions, both social and moral, that doomed the youth and the elegant and beguiling Edwardian sunset that enveloped him.

By the time the character-narration reveals the crisis of Leo's feelings about continuing to deliver letters, the time-present narration's scenes are likely to have accumulated sufficiently for one to discern the outlines of the story they tell. Certainly, the basic terms of causality are in place, but a good deal remains to be disclosed in both narrations and in their interaction. In one sense the meaning of Leo's present is defined by the loss of all that the past seems to promise. But as the dual narrations make clear, past and present cannot really be confined to different realms. What were parallel threads have intertwined, as Losey said. There are both boundaries and no boundaries at all in Leo's experience. In the interaction of the narrations, causes and effects are not by any means irrelevant, but they belong to linearity, to time divided. From the very first sequence the film subverts this conception of time – not because it is irrelevant, but because it is inadequate, too simple an explanation of a whole life.

In the final section, the structure and narration of *The Go-Between* become even more complex, and therein lies the film's subtlest, most far-reaching confrontation with the conception of time. The dual narrations, both third person and first; interactive time periods, one golden, the other gray and bleak, multiple voice-overs from both narrations; two disparate versions of Leo – these have defined the boy's world and prepared for the adult's remarkable encounter with Marian, which is the climax of the film. Time-present, confined until now to discontinuous fragments that seemingly interrupted the past, begins to command a larger, more extended place. Despite this reversal, however, time-past is not altogether subordinated. With accelerating frequency its images and, importantly, its voices are intercut with those of the present as the time-past narration moves toward its own climactic moment when Leo is ruthlessly forced to confront at last the mystery he has sought to comprehend and resolve. Ironically, the mounting urgency of the narration of the past intensifies one's sense of the buried emotion in the measured narration of time-present in which Leo will finally meet Marian again.

The use of voice-overs, which is significant throughout the film, becomes particularly insistent and telling in the last stages as the two narrations converge. Repeatedly linking the parallel narrations with voices from one period heard over images from the other, the voices, particularly those of both Leos, come to possess a unity of their own, forming a coherent narrational level on which the two Leos coexist. Thus, the voice of young Leo over the time-present cemetery scene may well be understood as the older Leo's recollection of a youthful comment that is deeply ironic in retrospect, but one may also begin to associate the adult's voice-overs with the boy's. This dimension of the film becomes even more complex when voices other than the young or adult Leo are heard. The voice-over accompanying the elder Leo's arrival at the station in the second time-present scene, for example, is that of Mrs. Maudsley explaining to young Leo his mother's proscription against him swimming. As the scene of the arrival at the station continues, other voices from a slightly later past moment are heard in an exchange between young Leo and one of the Maudsley sons, who asks why Leo is taking his bathing suit to a swimming party if he is forbidden to swim. The image of the arrival scene is then succeeded by one from the past, showing the party from the Hall walking toward the river carrying their bathing suits. These two time-past voice-overs, then, precede the images of the swimming sequence to which they belong. And in the most unusual instance of all, the adult Leo and Marian are heard twice in voice-overs repeating the same words — once in time-past and later in time-present — before the images of the scene in which they actually meet.

In the narration of time-present, the last section of the film is anticipated as early as the fourth time-present scene in which the adult Leo looks from a distance at the unidentified house that will prove to be the elderly Marian's. Later, immediately after the cricket match and celebration, when Leo learns from Marcus that Marian is engaged to Hugh, another time-present scene shows a young man (in a medium long shot) walking past the same house. The older Leo enters the frame, moving toward him until he sees Leo and turns in acknowledgment. Still later, after a time-past scene of young Leo bidding farewell to Ted in his expectation of leaving the Maudsleys and Brandham Hall, there is a second version of this scene of Leo and the young man. This time, shown from a different angle and with the two characters moving in a slightly different physical pattern, the young man hesitates as Leo approaches him. It is over this image that one first hears the voices of the older Marian and Leo before the scene of their meeting. She says: "So you met my grandson. Does he remind you of anyone?" Leo is heard replying: "Of course. Ted Burgess." And Marian says, "That's it. That's it. He does," as the scene concludes and an image of the Norfolk countryside follows. After a series of time-past scenes, including Leo joining the family for breakfast on his birthday, there appears another time-present scene at the site of the house. In an extreme long shot, the figures of the young man and Leo, barely distinguishable in the background, are shown shaking hands.

These four scenes, apparently presented in their story order, narrate a single event – Leo's meeting with Marian's grandson – but the narration raises several issues. First of all, the radically different camera distances and angles, even more than the separation of the images, infuse the event with an extreme discontinuity. One's experience of classical narration, which emphasizes continuity, is effectively contradicted by a narration that undercuts any sense of the event as internally coherent. Moreover, the temporal relationship of this encounter with the grandson to the eventual meeting between Leo and Marian is ambiguous. Does the encounter precede Marian's request that Leo be her go-between once more, or does it narrate his acquiescence to her call to carry one last message? The voices-over of Leo and Marian accompanying the third shot suggest that this encounter with the grandson is not the one for which Marian has summoned him. But given the complexity of time-present narration, particularly its atemporality, one cannot be certain. Attempting to resolve this issue proves crucial, however, for Leo's response to Marian's request is what the entire discourse has been leading to. Will Leo carry her message? Would carrying it constitute, ironically, a reentry into life because its import is hope and love? Or is it only that Leo's life still belongs to Marian? Can she alone command him after all these loveless years?

These questions are further complicated by the dual narrations, for the last shot of the encounter with the grandson is accompanied by yet another voice-over from the past. In this instance, in a line referring to the threat of rain for Leo's birthday celebration, one hears Mrs. Maudsley say, "It seems that all will be well for Leo's birthday." But, of course, the climax of the birthday dinner is not a celebration of Leo; it is Mrs. Maudsley's frantic dragging of the boy into the rain to confirm her own worst fears about Marian and Ted (Figure 35). The intersection of the voices from the birthday with the last shot of Leo meeting the grandson links the two events and prefigures the far more disturbing intersection of the confrontation scene with the lovers and Leo's final meeting with Marian. Indeed, the threads of the two narrations – both the voice-overs and the images – are woven together ever more tightly as the climactic meeting approaches.

Like the narration of the meeting with the grandson, the three shots showing the older Leo arriving at Marian's house and waiting to be announced to the now aged Lady Trimingham are widely separated in the discourse. In addition, their proper story sequence is reversed. The first presents Leo in Marian's sitting room, where one sees the man's face for the first time. This brief scene, which occurs somewhat after the midpoint in the film, is embedded in the time-past narration of the community hall festivities after the cricket match, where Ted, with Marian's accompaniment, sings "Take a Pair of Sparkling Eyes." Ted's song continues in voice-over

Figure 34. As Leo sings, the Union Jack with its red stripes makes a cross behind him and marks the boy as a potential victim. (Courtesy Weintraub Entertainment Ltd.)

Figure 35. An angry Mrs. Maudsley drags Leo through the rain to discover Marian and Ted in their trysting place. (Courtesy Weintraub Entertainment Ltd.)

Figure 36. During his last ride to Brandham Hall, the adult Leo's lifeless face expresses the sense of loss and pathos that haunt the ending of *The Go-Between*. (Courtesy Weintraub Entertainment Ltd.)

with the time-present scene. The second shot, which appears immediately after Ted orders Leo to leave because he refuses to carry another letter, shows the older Leo being led into the sitting room by the housekeeper. In voice-over young Leo is heard speaking the words of a letter to his mother requesting that he be allowed to return home immediately because "I am not enjoying myself here." This voice-over might speak also for the adult Leo's discomfiture at the prospect of meeting Marian again. The final shot, which appears in the midst of a brief time-past scene showing the boy sitting alone and troubled, presents Leo waiting at Marian's front door and then being greeted by the housekeeper, who leads him upstairs to the sitting room. Reversing the chronology of the story events, the third-person narration's subjectivizing of time here suggests a reluctance to confront Marian, expressing perhaps Leo's subconscious desire to back out of the meeting.

Because of the parallel narrations, the time-present scenes of Leo approaching his reunion with Marian are implicitly compared to time-past scenes of the boy's increasing anxiety over his role as go-between. As the character-narration moves toward its own climax, Leo struggles to extricate himself from his confusing position. Unfortunately, to his letter asking to come home early, Leo's mother responds (in a voice-over of her letter) that such an abrupt departure would be "ungrateful to Mrs. Maudsley." When his attempt to comfort Marian and counsel her to marry Ted fails to resolve Marian's problems or his own divided loyalties, Leo resorts again to his magic. In the middle of the night, he goes to the old garden, tears out the poisonous belladonna, and makes a potion from its berries, seeking perhaps to exorcise its sinister influence or to turn its power to advantage in resolving both his dilemma and Marian's. Leo soon knows that even this sorcery fails when Marian tries to force him to carry another message to Ted. This time Mrs. Maudsley catches sight of the note that Marian struggles to slip into Leo's jacket. Insisting that he walk in the garden with her, Mrs. Maudsley skillfully traps Leo in his (and Marian's) lies and tries to make the boy turn over the note. In this atmosphere of conspiracy and confusion, of moral compromise and increasing suspicions, Leo is given his birthday party.

The time-past scenes of the aborted birthday party followed by the discovery of the lovers divide the final meeting with Marian, which begins with a voice-over repeating the lines about seeing her grandson. Marian's attitude seems to confirm the endurance of the aristocratic code that Trimingham once expressed to the boy: "Nothing is ever a lady's fault." Marian is as self-centered and irresponsible as ever, having distilled from those tragic events a romanticized view of her affair and Leo's role as go-between. She tells Leo that she believes her grandson has some sort of grudge against her. He wants to marry a nice girl but won't. "I think he feels," she says, "he's under some sort of spell or curse... Now this is where you come in... You know what really happened... Tell him, tell him everything just as it happened... Every man should get married... You ought to have married. You're all dried up inside; I can tell that. Don't you feel any need of love? Speak to him. Tell him there's no spell or curse except an unloving heart." The reason Leo has returned to the sites of the past is now clear, and Marian's ongoing insensitivity to the price he has paid for his youthful affection and trust is appallingly evident. That she should ask Leo if he feels no need of love and advise him that an unloving heart is the only curse are more poignant than ironic. Marian created this man she so easily assesses and criticizes, and she shows not the slightest awareness of her role.

Following the discovery scene with the lovers, the last half of Marian's conversation with Leo is a sustained monologue addressed to the silent man seated opposite her in the dimly lit room. The monologue, which actually begins over the last moments of the discovery scene, continues even as the images of Marian and Leo are intercut with others from several different temporal instances, the last being Leo's drive to the now apparently abandoned Hall. Marian's voice-over begins: "You came out of the blue to make us happy. And we made you happy, didn't we? We trusted you with our great treasure. You might never have known what it was. You might have gone through life without knowing. Isn't that so?" The images accompanying these lines suddenly present the only time-past scene to be repeated, showing Leo and Marcus at the beginning of that summer skirting by Marian dressed in white and lying in a hammock. Now, in the light of Marian's declaration about the spell or curse of a loveless heart, this moment when young Leo seemed first to fall under her spell is especially telling. Moments later, between shots showing the older Leo's ashen face as he sits listening to Marian explain her plans for him, there is a brief scene, so still that it seems almost a freeze frame, depicting Ted's suicide. Recalling an earlier occasion when Leo saw Ted cleaning his gun at the same table, this image, intruding in the middle of her injunction to Leo that he tell the grandson "everything just as it was," certainly qualifies Marian's version of the past. As a prelude to her final request, the self-deluding Marian asks Leo to "remember how you loved taking our messages. Bringing us together and making us happy."

In the final lines of Hartley's novel, the epilogue allows for a cautiously affirmative note, the suggestion that perhaps in a reenactment of his youthful role Leo may at last be a go-between whose service brings life rather than death. The older Leo describes his ambivalent feelings:

> A foreigner in the world of the emotions, ignorant of their language but compelled to listen to it, I turned into the street. With every step I marvelled more at the extent of Marian's self-deception. Why then was I moved by what she had said? Why did I half wish that I could see it all as she did? And why should I go on this preposterous errand? I hadn't promised to and I wasn't a child, to be ordered about. My car was standing by the public call-box; nothing easier than to ring up Ted's grandson and make my excuses...
>
> But I didn't, and hardly had I turned in at the lodge gates, wondering how I should say what I had come to say, when the south-west prospect of the Hall, long hidden from my memory, sprang into view. (1984, 310–11)

However tentative the prospects in the novel for Leo's reentry into life, they exceed those of the film, which ends with the painful conversation between Leo and Marian, who has kept her illusions intact.

Like the camera moving through the rainy glass in the film's first image, Leo Colston has moved through the fatal, arrogant beauty of the past and its tragic conflicts of privilege and passion. Unlike the Leo of the novel, who half wishes "that I could see it all as she did" and who clearly carries out Marian's "preposterous errand," the film's Leo returns to the Hall without any indication that he is reenacting his role as go-between. Commenting on the ending, Losey told Ciment that Leo "has finally understood what his life has been and has put things back in perspective.... It's a belated catharsis. The old man finally refuses to allow himself to be used" (1985, 304). Losey's comment suggests a resolved, cathartic ending based on Leo's understanding and his refusal to carry Marian's message. "What is important about the ending," Losey said, "is that he doesn't pass on the message" (316). Nonetheless, the film's final sequence makes for a dark conclusion. Following a series of close-ups of Leo's face, almost ghostly in its lack of expression (Figure 36), one sees, as Marian's monologue continues, the last image of Leo through the rain-spattered car window on which the reflection of the Hall seems imprinted on his lifeless face. A sense of loss, of ironic pathos, haunts the ending. Leo's tragedy might have been avoided had he been either younger and more innocent or older and more experienced. But poised as he was between childhood and the first stirrings of those emotions and drives that would have led him to maturity, Leo became the victim of a world of adults who used him with little regard for his feelings and whose abuse of his trust ruined his life.

In the narration of The Go-Between, neither past nor present prevails. Their threads intertwine, and the tragedy of Leo Colston's life stands revealed. Although the loss of innocence is often poignant, the fact that this boy – open, sensitive, loving, vulnerable – should become this man – empty, unloving, cut off from human warmth – is doubly sad. The theme of time, for all its fascination for Losey and Pinter, and the richness and complexity of its role in the film, is not an end in itself. Rather, it is time in a particular man's life that is annihilated – not just an interest in time, but the meaning of time in Leo Colston's life that is the film's goal. Finally there is only one Leo, and his story as boy and man, his eager trust freely given and shockingly betrayed, his loving childhood and his loveless old age are what compel Losey and Pinter's attention and dominate the film.[3]

One of Losey's interests in The Go-Between, he told Ciment, came from his belief that "there are many traces of the society of that time remaining in society today" (1985, 304). He also identified "observation of characters, a very acute awareness of class dynamics and contradictions" as among the interests he shared with Pinter (242). Given the place and consequences of social class in the closed world of Hartley's story, Losey's interest in making the film might seem to confirm the view of him as a filmmaker of rigid social conscience, more interested in his characters' arguments than in their lives. But the film that Losey and Pinter have made from Hartley's novel focuses not so much on the social forces that bind the characters as on their passions and conflicts and on the emotional desolation that engulfs one man. Clearly, abuses of privilege in a society where rank carries not just influence but the power to force others to do one's bidding is a theme in *The Go-Between*, as it is in *King and Country* and *The Servant*.

When Ciment commented to Losey that none of the characters in *The Go-Between* was dislikable, that he showed great compassion for his characters, Losey responded: "I'm glad you sensed that because that's what I feel about people and that's what I want to demonstrate. But it's sometimes interpreted as indifference. People aren't either good or bad, they're both at the same time" (1985, 311). Marian, to be sure, is not only thoughtless but cruel in her assumptions about Leo as both a youth and an older man. Mrs. Maudsley, too, cruelly uses her rank and position to punish a child who, being an outsider of lower rank, she seems to blame for the crisis in her privileged but doomed world. Even Hugh, for all his good-natured fondness for Leo, fails to see how vulnerable the boy is. If one can argue that Hugh has no idea of Leo's role as Marian and Ted's go-between, his conversation with Leo and Mr. Maudsley in the smoking room scene suggests that he is not entirely unaware of the threat Ted poses to him. And given Leo's questions in the same scene about Ted and about the consequences of a jealous love affair among adults, Hugh seems at least inattentive to the boy's uncertainties. But for all that *The Go-Between* exposes of the painful and hypocritical inequities of class, all of its characters, not just Leo, are shown in their human complexity. If their doubts and sufferings do not excuse their failures, Marian and Ted, Hugh, and even Mrs. Maudsley are nonetheless poignant. Like so many of Losey's characters, they are victims all.

Losey's insight into his characters is apparent in his comments to Ciment about casting in the film:

> Originally we wanted to do *The Go-Between* with an unknown girl, because the girl really ought to have been about 18, 19 years old . . . to make it work the way it should have. . . . The farmer too should have been very young. It really was a story of very young lovers who were using a little boy who was only slightly younger than they were.

They were on opposite sides of adolescence, of pubescence, and that's the way I wanted to do it but for reasons of finance we were quite unable to do it. (1985, 240)

It detracts not at all from the sensitive performances of Julie Christie and Alan Bates to see the point of Losey's assessment. There would likely have been another kind of poignance and different emotional nuances had the lovers been so young. Nonetheless, Christie and Bates, who are actually in only four scenes together, make palpable the lovers' passion and urgency and their dilemma in a world that refuses to allow such emotions to cross social barriers. What is especially telling about Losey's view is its emphasis on the characters' youth rather than their different classes.

So far as social issues are concerned, the gulf separating Marian's world from Ted's is not fundamentally different from that between Tony's and Barrett's in *The Servant*. In both films class differences play a decisive role in the unfolding conflict and are exposed for their false values and hypocrisy. In neither film, however, do Losey and Pinter sacrifice the drama of the human conflict in order to expose and criticize the social. So, too, in *King and Country* Hamp's and Hargreaves's fates wear a human face whatever the corrupt values and hypocritical forces that engulf them. The social critic that Losey was in his earlier films has grown in his understanding and compassion for characters caught in conflicts that are often harsh and cruel. It is a measure of Losey's growth, and the fruitfulness of his collaboration with Pinter, that the considerable formal complexity of *The Go-Between*, its brilliant exploration of subjectivity and time, serves to reveal a drama of human loss and suffering. Time in its wholeness, like social prejudices in their narrowness, is a rich theme precisely because the lives of Leo and the others are both moving and worth remembering. Losey's later films do not forsake this understanding, but in *The Go-Between* he achieves perhaps its most memorable expression.

6

"The Arrival of
Strangers"

The Romantic Englishwoman

By turns wry and bitter, *The Romantic Englishwoman* is a sexual comedy,
a social satire, even a domestic melodrama – with a curious thread of the
crime thriller woven in for good measure. It is also a gloss on themes and
formal elements that preoccupied Losey throughout his artistic life. He
compared the film, which was written by Thomas Wiseman and Tom Stoppard from a novel by Wiseman, to *The Prowler, Eve,* and *Accident,* saying:
"It deals with an impossible domestic situation in which a bourgeois life
encases people and they don't get out of it" (Ciment 1985, 341). True
enough, but it also differs from the films Losey compares it to, particularly
in tone, for *The Romantic Englishwoman* is a kind of high-wire act, treading
a fine line with its shifting tones always threatening to upset a precarious
balance. In its attitudes toward its characters, the film comes close to reflecting the detachment Losey was often accused of, but that is a function
of its reflexivity, its self-knowing wit, rather than mere distance on Losey's
part. A self-conscious commentary on its own narrative strategies is as much
a deliberate theme of the film as those that arise from its story. The principal
characters include a wealthy popular novelist, Lewis Fielding (Michael
Caine), his frustrated but adventurous wife, Elizabeth (Glenda Jackson), on
whom he projects relentless fantasies of betrayal, and the handsome, mysterious young foreigner, Thomas Hursa (Helmut Berger), who intrudes on
their uneasy marriage at Lewis's all too perverse invitation. From beginning
to end, the film "talks" about itself as a story about stories, about its
characters as types, and about its various genre legacies even as it trades
shamelessly and wittily in the currency of these very genres and types. The
result is a mordant comedy that ends not amusingly but sadly and that
leaves a viewer more than a little uncertain how to respond to dilemmas
that are at once clever and dangerous.

More than most of Losey's films, *The Romantic Englishwoman* had a relatively untroubled production history. Shot immediately after *Galileo,* Losey's film for Ely Landau's short-lived American Film Theatre series based on the Brecht play he had staged nearly three decades earlier, *The Romantic Englishwoman* is a film about which Losey later maintained he had little to comment on. "I was less personally involved than on some of the other films," he told Richard Combs. "I didn't have to conduct the same kind of personal battles, and consequently I found that I could cut much more ruthlessly" (1975, 141). Also, he said to Ciment: "I wasn't passionate about it but it's true that I saw something of interest and value.... And I rather liked shooting it" (1985, 340). These comments focus noticeably on the production circumstances, Losey's freedom from many of the struggles that so often attended his efforts, rather than the film itself. In this sense the film was obviously among his least passionate, just as he said, but intellect rather than passion (however passionate its characters) is in fact typical of the film. Even so, the conclusion in which husband and wife return to the life they lived before, despite their sometimes comic, sometimes dramatic, and always ineffectual attempts to break free, is not without poignance. Lewis and Elizabeth Fielding hardly summon the sympathy and compassion that belong to Leo Colston, Hamp and Hargreaves, or perhaps even Stephen, but the film does not merely skewer their follies and indulgences or those of their world. The Fieldings are trapped by their own inability to conceive a larger than bourgeois life, and the final scenes center as much on their real pain as on its emblems.

Associated once again with Daniel Angel, who produced *King and Country,* Losey worked for a time with the novel's author, Thomas Wiseman, who "did an original script with me which was interesting and good in many ways, but like many novelists he was inclined to put into the script purple descriptions that are not so easily translated into the visual" (Combs 1975, 140). Whatever the limits of Wiseman's descriptions, the controlling premise of his novel would also raise problems for the adaptation; for Lewis Fielding, who is himself a novelist, is posited as writing the very novel one is reading. His wife is thus not only a character in her own right, but one whose frustrated desires Lewis seeks to control by making her also a character in his fiction. This premise is maintained in the film, but the conceit of reading a novel by a novelist, a literary reflexivity, is transformed; in the film Lewis is writing a screenplay that allows him to "recreate" Elizabeth's recent trip alone to Baden-Baden in the light of his all-consuming fears and jealous fantasies. While the film was in postproduction, Losey remarked:

What interested me most about [the novel] were the various points of view – the fantasy of the husband about his wife, the fantasy of the wife about herself, plus the catalyst of the poet, who says very little but is the only one who really has an articulate philosophy. . . . Tom Stoppard took it [Wiseman's script from his novel] and treated it with a good deal of irreverence and made it quite funny. He hardly changed the structure, except he injected a bit more of the adventurer into the poet, but he largely rewrote the dialogue. It's a pretty bitter comedy of domestic life, and it could be like a more conventional *Discreet Charm of the Bourgeoisie.* (140)

Losey's interest in "various points of view" attests to his ongoing concern for storytelling, for narration, for forms of subjectivity that are crucial to an understanding of the complex structure and characterization in his films. Playing as it does with various genres and storylines, *The Romantic Englishwoman* is vulnerable to attack for its apparent lack of unity, its seemingly confused intentions. Its title might point to Elizabeth as the protagonist and her story as the focus of the film. Whether she can have "her story," however, is problematic and a central concern in the film. Conflict centers around Lewis's need to narrate (and thereby control Elizabeth whether through his script or by way of creating situations through his insistence that Thomas Hursa stay with them) and Elizabeth's need to enact her own freedom outside of the home and against the various scripted roles that define and confine her. Struggling to free herself from Lewis's fantasies, she ultimately takes flight with Thomas, an act that at once defies Lewis and enacts the very fantasy he has feared and written into his screenplay. Will Elizabeth be allowed her own desire, her own subjectivity, or can she only play a part in other people's stories, be they her husband's jealous fantasies or Thomas Hursa's con-game thriller? This was neither the first time nor the last that Losey focused on women and their struggles within sexist societies. Indeed, in his last two films, *La Truite* and *Steaming*, he dealt with women characters and their quest for freedom, power, and self-determination more fully than one could anticipate from his earlier films.

For all the irreverence and wit of Stoppard's dialogue, the issues at stake are serious, having to do with Elizabeth's inchoate yearning for personal freedom and identity as opposed to Lewis's possessiveness and jealous determination to control her. But whether the issue is freedom or control, choice or responsibility, fantasy seems the principal recourse of both characters. Sometimes narrated and at others only implied, fantasies continually intervene in the couple's contentious relationship and often threaten to define it altogether. Does Elizabeth really desire freedom, or merely fantasize romantic escape? Does Lewis genuinely love Elizabeth and understand and worry about her restless vulnerability, or does he only fantasize equally romantic betrayal because, as he once says, "I have to have everything in its place"? "The realm of possibility is a terrible country," Lewis declares somewhat drunkenly during a dinner party at a restaurant with their film producer friend Herman. "What if such-and-such were the case? What if the person you love is a liar?" he asks. "You say, it won't happen to me . . . But others are not so lucky. Hypochondriacs, paranoids, novelists — who say it will happen to me. The truth will blow up in my face one day, and that will be the end of my precarious existence. The tiles will fall from the roof, the paint will peel from the window frame, the lawn run riot, and the fruit will go rotting in the fruit bowl." A perverse fantasy, yes, and a very funny one as Michael Caine plays it, that reveals a good deal about Lewis, including the fact that he is not un-self-knowing; and also a thinly veiled threat to Elizabeth, his real audience that evening in the restaurant, that he will not accept her uneventful account of her trip alone to Baden-Baden, with which the film begins.

Elizabeth's sojourn in the German resort, what may or may not have happened there, and its consequences drive the story of *The Romantic Englishwoman*. Not only is Lewis obsessed by suspicion that Elizabeth had an affair while on holiday, but to make matters worse, her putative lover, Thomas Hursa, the handsome young man she met there who seems less the poet his passport claims than a gigolo of mysterious background and intentions, is about to arrive on the Fieldings' doorstep. Lewis not only invites Hursa to tea (without consulting Elizabeth), but to dinner afterward, and then, to Elizabeth's astonishment, to stay overnight. One devious invitation leads to another, and before long Hursa is installed as a long-term houseguest and even works for "pocket money" as Lewis's secretary handling correspondence. Elizabeth is outraged at Lewis's game. He claims he merely wants to observe Thomas as the basis for a character in the screenplay he is writing for Herman. Elizabeth rightly perceives that Lewis is also conducting a test of her declaration that nothing at all happened with Thomas in Baden-Baden. Lewis seems determined to have Thomas in his home and under his eye in order to confront Elizabeth and, presumably, force her to confess. Reflecting the psychological, social, and moral issues of the film, all of this is outrageous; it also sets up an instance of the multiple levels of reflexivity that give the film its special temper.

Well before Thomas's arrival, but after receiving a letter from him mailed in Paris, Lewis interrogates Elizabeth in his study, whose walls are papered with countless photographs of her face in various expressions:

LEWIS: What is he [Hursa] like?
ELIZABETH: Young...and a poet.
LEWIS: Was it that night I phoned?
ELIZABETH: Was what?
LEWIS: You said, "The lift is coming." Is that when you met?
ELIZABETH: That's right.
LEWIS: Tell me about him?
ELIZABETH: Why?
LEWIS: I want to write him in.
ELIZABETH: Jesus wept!
LEWIS: Well, did he show you his poetry?
ELIZABETH: In the lift?
LEWIS: How do you know he is a poet?
ELIZABETH: Because he told me.
LEWIS: "What floor do you want? By the way, I'm a poet." I was calling your room.
ELIZABETH: I was in the bath.
LEWIS: In my version they'll screw.
ELIZABETH: In the lift.
LEWIS: How did you guess?
ELIZABETH: I know your mind.

The scene reveals Lewis's obsession with what might have happened in the lift and his plan to incorporate Hursa into his screenplay. Also evident is Elizabeth's perceptive view of Lewis ("I know your mind" – a claim, almost an allegation, both make at one time or another) and her exasperation with his game of turning her sins, real or imagined, into his art. Besides its place in the story, this scene also underlines the theme of the problematic relation of art and life, which recurs throughout the film. Well before this moment, however, the film has introduced the reflexivity that folds itself into the discourse, for the long initial segment, including Elizabeth's trip to Baden-Baden and various scenes of Lewis's response to it, has already established the intricate ways story and discourse comment on one another. Moreover, the extent to which the narrative has begun to invoke various film genres (and familiar traces of Losey's visual style) constitute still further comments that will recur.

The long opening shot (in part behind the credits), showing a train window beyond which snow-covered mountains slip by, holds the reflection of a woman passenger whose image alternately appears and disappears against the dark and light background of the landscape. As the landscape first absorbs and then reflects the figure, her image seems almost apparitional, that of a character who disappears at one moment as tantalizingly as she materializes in the next. When the train arrives at a border station, a second sequence briefly introduces a young man who speaks German fluently and whose luggage and passport are examined routinely by a German border official. This short sequence is followed by a return to a shot of the woman asleep in her seat. As the segment proceeds, scenes crosscut between the woman and the young man. He leaves his compartment and enters a washroom on the train, where he retrieves several packets of drugs hidden under the sink. The man's actions (and a darker musical score than the romantic orchestration that accompanied the first view of the woman), together with the doubling of the man's image in the washroom mirror, add to a suggestive, even ominous mood of the sort typical of stories of international crime and espionage. As the train enters Baden-Baden, the two characters' paths cross, and they eventually exchange glances when the woman tours the city in a carriage that twice passes the man on the road as she heads for her hotel. Later, the man hides the drugs in a drainpipe on the hotel roof, then amusingly steals a room service dinner and dines elegantly alone in the hotel garden, where he establishes a liaison with a wealthy older woman. The omniscient narration, coolly observant and apparently without comment, presents the incipient relationship between the unscrupulous and enterprising young man and the wryly observant woman traveller who is, of course, Elizabeth Fielding. Later, after the two characters exchange glances again, this time across a gaming table in the casino, the man follows Elizabeth back to the hotel, where she takes a phone call in the lobby from her husband, who has remained in England with their son. After the brief phone conversation, during which she refers to her dissatisfaction with her domestic life, Elizabeth tells Lewis that the lift has arrived in the lobby and hangs up. The scene then cuts to England and a view of Lewis, reflected in a mirror, showing him replacing the phone receiver. He tells the young au pair girl to go to bed and then retires to his study, where he fantasizes an erotic encounter that he fears Elizabeth is having in the lift (Figure 37).

In Baden-Baden, Elizabeth is indeed riding the lift with Thomas Hursa. Striking up a conversation, he reminds her that she saw him on the road

122

without stopping and introduces himself as a poet. Elizabeth notes wryly that he got "picked up anyway" and that his life as a "poet" must be hard. "These women are difficult," says Hursa. "If they weren't, they wouldn't have to pay, perhaps." When Elizabeth notices that she is on the wrong floor, she and Hursa take the lift down; an overhead shot shows the descending lift with Hursa crossing over to Elizabeth, possibly assuming an intimate stance reminiscent of the seducer in Lewis's character-narration of his jealous fantasy. Another cut to Lewis phoning Elizabeth a half hour later leaves open the possibility of a sexual encounter between Elizabeth and Hursa, but she tells Lewis she fell asleep in the bath. However possible, the seduction in the lift seems unlikely; nevertheless, Lewis's obsessive jealousy leads to another brief post-telephone fantasy of his wife's supposed infidelity in the lift, a fantasy interrupted by their son's crying out for his absent mother.

As discrete sequences, the train and Baden-Baden scenes recall such genre films as Hitchcock's *To Catch a Thief* and Stanley Donen's *Charade*, romantic comedy-thrillers whose charming leading players, adventurous plots, and exotic locales promise both light entertainment and excitement and witty resolutions where couples are happily and stylishly united. But the interpolation of the scenes of Lewis (and his fantasies) in England, though it doesn't necessarily block the thriller possibilities, raises other issues pointing in the direction of domestic melodrama. This seems at least partially confirmed when the opening sequence in Baden-Baden is abruptly terminated with a cut to a brief long shot of a large modern house, followed by an interior shot of two men talking. The setting is the Fieldings' home, and one of the men, speaking with a German accent, says, "She feels that by getting away by herself she will get to know herself." The other man, Lewis, begins, "sounds like the kind of thing Elizabeth . . . " The first man continues: "So this woman . . . buys a ticket to self-discovery. Rome, Paris – doesn't matter to her, doesn't matter to me. I can shoot it anywhere. It's a psychological story of the New Woman." Herman, the film producer, is trying to persuade Lewis Fielding to write the script of the story he has just summarized. "I think it's a very boring idea," Lewis responds. "It's also pretentious and derivative. But mostly it's boring. Why don't you turn it into a thriller?" "Wonderful," Herman agrees. "I'll leave it up to you." Lewis declines on the grounds that he is about to begin a new novel and then adds plaintively, "Anyway, I can't work. I want to see Elizabeth."

Herman's description of his proposed new film is clearly ironic, for, unaware that Elizabeth is in Baden-Baden, he summarizes a story with obvious similarities to her arrival in the resort. Of course, nothing in Elizabeth's

Figure 37. One of Lewis Fielding's dark, jealous imaginings of Elizabeth's supposed infidelity in Baden-Baden, in *The Romantic Englishwoman*. (Courtesy Dial Trading Ltd.)

journey and her stay in Baden-Baden, as the viewer has seen it, requires its being understood as comparable to Herman's story. In other words, nothing requires one to suppose Elizabeth a New Woman, or on a voyage of self-discovery. Why, then, is the comparison likely? First of all, in the opening sequence, exposition about the woman's identity and motives has been suppressed by the narration, leaving one in the dark. Second, genre conventions and their typical ways of explaining characters are readily available to remedy this lack. For the viewer, the process is almost unconscious, but it will eventually be tested by the narration's reflexivity. On another level, also reflexive, clichés such as "a ticket to self-discovery" expose Herman's proposed film as having less to do with the New Woman than with an old genre. His story is the stuff of "women's films" of the thirties and forties – Bette Davis in *Now, Voyager,* for example – rather than the experience of a contemporary woman defining her place in a world much changed and changing still. (Herman's declaration that the locale "doesn't matter to her, doesn't matter to me. I can shoot it anywhere" only underlines the impersonal, formulaic nature of the project.) On the face of it, Lewis's dismissal of Herman's idea seems altogether justified; pretentious, derivative, and boring it certainly is. Lewis's tone, however, betrays an unacknowledged

Figure 38. Reminiscent of distorting images in *The Servant*, this reflection shows the Fieldings and Hursa during a tense, argumentative supper. (Courtesy Dial Trading Ltd.)

Figure 39. Reading Lewis's script, Elizabeth discovers that he has transcribed one of their private conversations directly into his "creative" work. (Courtesy Dial Trading Ltd.)

hostility that hints at more intimate concerns. Whatever its source, considerable anger resides in Lewis that will surface with increasing significance and self-destructiveness once Elizabeth returns home. For the moment, though, he masks his emotion by suggesting Herman convert his film into a thriller – a proposition both revealing and ironic.

The thriller genre hardly signifies a film more sophisticated than what Herman has proposed. Moreover, rather than matters psychological or social, the thriller's conventions and typical concerns of mystery, high adventure, and stylized romance require a move still further away than Herman's from any genuine consideration of issues important to women. Thus, when Lewis would merely substitute one (inappropriate) genre for another, the implied intellectual or artistic high ground of his criticism proves to be a sham. But at another level, the thriller genre that Lewis proposes accommodates what has just been narrated in the opening sequence, notably the gigolo and his drug smuggling. Herman's tale of the New Woman makes no provision for drug dealers or smugglers, whether gigolos or not. Lewis's proposal, however unintentionally, does make room for such characters. He prefers a gilded adventure that eschews significance, or even a predictable melodrama, to the unsettling questions raised by Elizabeth's journey.[1]

The film's first act concludes with Elizabeth's return home and Hursa's quick exit from Baden-Baden. Having dismissed Lewis's second phone call with her announcement that she is coming home, she takes a plane back to England. Meanwhile, Hursa has troubles of his own. Entering the hotel lobby with his expensive older woman, he suddenly recognizes another man who is approaching the concierge; Hursa makes an excuse and returns to the woman's room. Having checked the drugs he had placed in the drainpipe on the roof only to discover that the packets have been destroyed by the heavy rain now falling, Hursa urgently packs a few belongings, steals some money from the woman's purse, and slips out of the hotel. The viewer therefore realizes long before either of the Fieldings that Thomas has his own reasons to seek an out-of-the-way refuge. That his motives for following up on his acquaintance with Elizabeth should coincide with Lewis's rampant jealousy is not the least of the film's ironies.

Lewis's frustrations turn nasty when his jealousy focuses on Elizabeth's friend, Isabel (Kate Nelligan). From his study window, he views Elizabeth and Isabel's meeting in the gazebo, a visual foreshadowing of his view of the sexual tryst between Elizabeth and Hursa later in the film. Lewis proceeds to a vicious and unprovoked attack against Isabel. His motives for lashing out at her certainly include his sense that he has been unable to discover the truth (although, in fact, he has probably learned all there is to know) about Elizabeth's activities in Baden-Baden. The bitter exchange between Lewis and Isabel coalesces around two issues – their mutual desire to know what Elizabeth might have done on her holiday and an assessment of the position of women in society. Isabel doesn't regard "a woman's destiny to be to sit at home and wash her husband's underpants." She sharply, if somewhat glibly, insists that "women are an occupied country." Lewis responds not by denying her assertions, but by declaring Isabel "the most boring woman in the world" and by judging her pronouncements to be the commonplace platitudes of a commercial gossip. Lewis's ad hominem arguments and his final accusation that Isabel is imputing her own low standards of fidelity to Elizabeth reveal more about his insecurities ("She practically accused you of having an affair in Baden," he shouts at Elizabeth) than they do Isabel's inadequacies. Nevertheless, the issues of women's victimization and repression and their rights to their own desire and to a freedom and destiny beyond wifely roles are addressed, though hardly resolved, in the remainder of the film.

In bed that evening an apparently amused Lewis tells Elizabeth about his film script for Herman. Playing on what he supposes are the parallels between his script and Elizabeth's recent trip, he says that "it's about discontent" and asks if she is discontented. Her answer is especially significant as it not only ends this scene, but is repeated at the beginning of the following scene in Lewis's study. Elizabeth says, "I would be, but I don't feel I have the right." When the next day she reads aloud her answer reproduced in Lewis's script, she responds: "Bloody hell, do I get a percentage?" (Figure 39). In his response ("You already get half. What more do you want?") Lewis denies her right to her own words because she is financially dependent on him. Ironically, Lewis's habit of using the life around him in an unmediated way in his script will eventually backfire on him when life, somewhat stage-managed by him, all too closely comes to follow his script.

The confrontation between the couple in Lewis's study constitutes a crucial scene in the film. Each character offers a revelatory set piece that presages, in Lewis's case, the narrative trajectory and denouement of the film one is watching, and in Elizabeth's case, her view of the central issues surrounding her identity and self-image as a woman:

ELIZABETH: So what's it [the film script] about?
LEWIS: It's about this ungrateful woman who is married to this man of great charm, brilliance, and integrity. She thinks he won't let her be herself,

and she feels stuck in a straightjacket when she ought to be out and about, taking the waters, and finding herself. So one day she ups and goes and finds herself out of her depth. But the husband comes and saves her and then she realizes that he's really a wonderful chap.

ELIZABETH: Does he play cricket for England, too?

LEWIS: I can't think of his line back to her.

ELIZABETH: No? . . . Perhaps I am who you think I am. So what the hell. David's fine. Your book sells ten thousand hard and a hundred thousand soft. The roof doesn't leak, the house is painted, the deep freeze is full to overflowing, and there is fruit on the sideboard. I have twenty-eight pairs of shoes in my wardrobe, eleven long dresses, and no knickers. I haven't been on a bus since 1959. I have an account at Harrods, a standing order to Oxfam. So what the bloody hell!

Elizabeth's bitter and comic summary obviously echoes Lewis's own litany of fears expressed in the restaurant scene.

In his wish-fulfilling summary of his script, Lewis casts the husband as hero and the wife as a confused ingrate in need of rescue. At one level, this quintessential male fantasy offers a possible interpretation of *The Romantic Englishwoman* itself; however, Lewis's glib and funny summary is not just incomplete, but misleading. Not surprisingly, the wife in his version comes to realize that her husband is "really a wonderful chap," but such an assessment is hardly ascribable to Elizabeth at the conclusion of the film. In fact, there is a radical shift in tone in the last section, for the anticipations of Lewis's script become an anguishing experience as they are played out by the Fieldings themselves. Moreover, the relationship of the script (Lewis's) within the script (the film one is watching) enlarges a number of complex issues that were introduced in the first scene between Lewis and Herman. Is Lewis prescient, or is he somehow responsible for authoring and bringing about, indeed, living out, his script? Is his supposed power merely an illusion that places him in a position to suffer and learn when the narrative in which he is only a character supersedes the narrative produced by his own rather feeble creative powers? Clearly, his script and *The Romantic Englishwoman* are alike and radically different.

Elizabeth's response to Lewis, both her words and actions, merits careful attention. What right, indeed, does she have to harbor discontent when her life is marked by such good fortune? Still, implicit in her description of their comfortable bourgeois life is her judgment on herself and a social structure that has, she feels, robbed her of any personal, self-defined identity. What she has determines who she is. She is, in other words, defined from without,

128

not from within. As both consumer and commodity, she has become an object among other objects. She cannot purchase a self; she can only witness and be paid for or pay for her own commodification as an object of exchange for men. Once Thomas arrives on the scene, however, this self-estimate is called into question. What threatens Lewis's world is not just the fear of betrayal, of cuckoldry, but the possibility that Elizabeth may have acted out her own desire. Women in Lewis's view, it would seem, have no right to desire; they can only be consumers or be consumed. This attitude is pointedly addressed on several occasions. First, a minor character in the restaurant scene obtusely asks Herman's beautiful female companion, a professor of philosophy at the Sorbonne, "What do you girls make a night?" And as Hursa commented on his own women clients: "These women are difficult. If they weren't they wouldn't have to pay, perhaps." Finally, something more than money is involved in the exchange that follows Lewis's discovery of Elizabeth and Hursa locked in an erotic embrace. Lewis says, almost venomously, to Hursa, "I know you never pay for anything, but this time you will." Elizabeth replies to herself as well as the men, "I'll pay."[2]

Elizabeth is aware by this time that her identity is the product of various social codes, a construct that needs deconstructing if she is ever to act from a personal sense of self and be able to generate her own story and her own subjectivity. The fact that the walls of Lewis's study are covered with multiple photographs of her disembodied head has emphasized her fragmented, reproducible image that objectifies her and turns her into a spectacle under her husband's constant view. At the very moment in the earlier scene when she delivers to Lewis her bitter tribute to her bourgeois life, she also begins to deface her image (Figure 40). As she talks of the reproduction of Lewis's latest book ("ten thousand hard and a hundred thousand soft"), she mocks her own multiple images by taking a pen and drawing eye glasses, wrinkles, and mustaches on the arty photographs. Just as she resists Lewis's attempt to turn her words into dialogue, Elizabeth here tries to retrieve her fetishized image. Her protests, however, in the scene in Lewis's study and then later in her almost frantic encounter with Hursa ("I don't expect you to love me") are more urgent than convincing. Elizabeth has first denied Lewis's fantasies and now confirmed them. But, in either instance, has she enacted her own self, or only imagined it? The film's final sequence of her flight with Thomas both sharpens this question and leaves it finally unanswered. Has Lewis really won, or was the game itself misconceived?

In a conversation only minutes after Thomas Hursa's arrival at the Fieldings' house in Weybridge, Lewis pointedly asks him about Baden-Baden and its clientele. Thomas allows that many cures are indeed sought, not all

Figure 40. Elizabeth defaces her own image as she delivers to Lewis her mocking tribute to their comfortable bourgeois life. (Courtesy Dial Trading Ltd.)

Figure 41. As he writes his script, Lewis's character-narration imagines the nude and symmetrically posed Elizabeth and Hursa conversing in a Baden-Baden spa in an image that reveals his overripe jealous fantasy. (Courtesy Dial Trading Ltd.)

Figure 42. *The Romantic Englishwoman* ends wth this shot of the grim-faced Fieldings enclosed in their car and staring at their house full of unwanted party guests. (Courtesy Dial Trading Ltd.)

of them from the spa's celebrated waters, and that, yes, bored wives are prominent among the seekers. To this Lewis remarks, with a studied disinterestedness, "Well, the place must attract a certain type of young man of easy disposition, tolerable appearance, and a shortage of cash." Not at all discomfited by the insinuation, Thomas laughs and says, "So you know it, then." The exchange marks Thomas's introduction to the game that Lewis has been playing compulsively since Elizabeth's holiday. Thomas's ease and his laugh should warn Lewis to beware. He cannot win this game, least of all against Thomas, whose complete lack of self-consciousness is proof against any rhetorical weapons Lewis might raise in the name of bourgeois values.

Hursa is a curious character. He is, of course, another of the intruders who so often appear in Losey's films, although Losey once said that "it's not a theme that I have chosen. . . . I haven't consciously gone and said 'I want to make pictures about lives that are disrupted by the arrival of strangers' " (Ciment 1985, 343). Strangers or intruders nonetheless claim a prominent place in the world of his films, and like most of them, Hursa is the catalyst of a fierce struggle for power in the world he enters, although power never seems his own object. His potency in the struggle, however, arises from sources quite unlike those of other such Losey characters – say, at one extreme, the fateful innocence of young Leo Colston in *The Go-Between* or, at the other, the sly and corrupt deference of Barrett in *The Servant*. Whatever Thomas may be, he is neither deferential nor innocent of worldly experience. Neither is he simply a catalyst. He plays a critical role in the angry contest between Lewis and Elizabeth, but this does not define him. True, his values are radically opposed to those of both the Fieldings, which the film quite ruthlessly exposes. As Losey himself has said of Thomas, "He's someone who's totally free of bourgeois life, whereas they're totally trapped in it" (Combs 1975, 140). But Thomas is not by any means a hero. Even what happens to him at the end when his mysterious pursuer from the drug smuggling transaction catches up with him is unclear. For that matter, the drug smuggling undercuts any view of Thomas as a kind of moralist or even simply a victim. One of the more perplexing questions posed by *The Romantic Englishwoman,* then, is what to make of Thomas.

Both Thomas and Elizabeth are reinvented by Lewis twice over as characters in his fictions – that is, as characters in Lewis's script as well as in the obsessive suspicions that inform it. Lewis may be said to have invented Thomas in yet another way also, for it was he who encouraged his visit and then invited him to stay, thus "casting" Thomas in a role that Lewis believes is already written. In one sense Thomas is a truth teller, not only because he says what he thinks, but more importantly because he understands what he thinks. His way of life, which Losey called anarchic, shocks less than his refusal to apologize for it. His clear eye for the self-deceptions of the world around him, however, and his willingness to state them may make him sound almost a moralist nonetheless. Compared with Lewis, who seems unable to make anything better of his declared love and desire for Elizabeth than relentless suspicion and impotent rage, Thomas is perhaps more appealing. But, then, candor as a measure of virtue has its limits. Something more is required; some capacity for giving is at stake. Ultimately that proves to be the test for all the principal characters in *The Romantic Englishwoman.* Eventually, as if in deliberate fulfillment of Lewis's presumptions, Elizabeth casts Thomas as a central character in a fantasy just as Lewis did before her. For Lewis he was a villain, an unprincipled seducer; for Elizabeth he would be a hero. But, of course, he is neither.

Losey's remark about being most interested in the various points of view in Wiseman's novel is reflected in the film's narration, which is intimately connected to its complexities of tone and different forms of subjectivity.

The overall narration is omniscient, although it bears traces of what David Bordwell would call authorial commentary and Kawin "perspectival presentation," an implied authorial perspective on what is shown. The film does not attempt to reproduce the novel's use of interior monologue, but Lewis is nonetheless the source of several instances of character-narration that present his fantasies, which are of two sorts. The first, Elizabeth being seduced by a stranger in the hotel lift in Baden-Baden, is triggered by her statement during Lewis's first phone call to her in the resort and his second call a few minutes later asking where she has been in the meantime. With nothing more to go on than his compulsive suspicion and her remark that she must hang up because the lift has arrived, he twice imagines Elizabeth passionately submitting to the stranger's advances. The third time his obsessive vision occurs is on his drive home from the docks where he had mistakenly gone to meet Elizabeth. The disorienting and obscure way these scenes are shown (the shifting light in the moving lift, the oblique angles of the moving camera) makes it difficult to be sure precisely what is happening. Whatever else, the dark images convey Lewis's state of mind – his fear, his resistence to seeing (knowing), his own guilt and shame, perhaps, at imagining his wife's infidelity and his cuckoldry. The second form of his fantasies narrates scenes from the screenplay he is writing in which he constructs additional encounters with the stranger. Once Thomas Hursa is ensconced in the Fieldings' house, however, he becomes the identifiable seducer in Lewis's script.

The two forms of Lewis's fantasies differ in a number of respects. However imaginary in origin and stylized in their expressionist images, the first two lift scenes might well be supposed part of the omniscient narration were it not for the weight of the convention of preceding each with an image of Lewis, suggesting that he is their likely character-narrator. The third instance, however, during Lewis's drive back from the dock, is immediately recognizable as a mindscreen. An image of Lewis driving in his car this time precedes the image in the lift; the viewer has seen him fantasize the same moment twice before; and there is no longer a plausible temporal anchor in the ongoing Baden-Baden segment. Lewis's screenplay fantasies, by contrast, are all firmly anchored in scenes showing him at work on the screenplay he has promised Herman. Moreover, their tone, which is highly artificial in image, action, and dialogue, and consistent from one instance to another, differs significantly from the scenes of Lewis's involuntary fears, which he narrates only to himself. By contrast, the screenplay's imagined scenes are anything but involuntary. They are in fact almost perversely willed as Lewis elaborates on his suspicions with extravagant suppositions and with versions of what Elizabeth has actually said in response to his none too subtle questions. Neither are they exactly narrated by Lewis only to himself. To be sure, even he apparently realizes their ludicrous extremes and tears out of his typewriter the pages on which he has written them. The very intent, even if aborted, of making a commercial fiction out of his fantasies casts them in quite different terms from his basically private fears, however. And Losey makes the most of this dual status both to reveal Lewis's character and to comment wryly on the problematic relationship of life and art.

Losey's treatment of this theme is witty rather than obviously serious, clever and playful both intellectually and formally rather than overtly philosophical. Doubtless this owes something to the collaboration with Stoppard, whose plays before and after *The Romantic Englishwoman* (his first screenplay) typically juggle a fascination with wordplay, intellectualized dilemmas, and a self-conscious theatricalization of ideas more than an interest in individual human character. But one of Losey's defining traits has always been a strong sense of irony. In his associations first with Pinter and then Stoppard, his sense of the complexity of characters, the contradictions of human action and reaction, are joined to his interest in the resources of language and self-conscious film form. When added to the fervor and insight of the social and political views that marked his films from the beginning, the result in *The Romantic Englishwoman* is an ironic comedy that grows increasingly dark and even desperate. Stoppard, like Losey, has sometimes been criticized for an apparent lack of interest in the purely human dimension of characters, and one can see traces of this impulse in the film they made together. But the treatment of Lewis's screenplay fantasies belies this criticism somewhat, for these scenes not only make explicit the theme of the relationship of art and life, but subtly (and comically) provide the viewer with insight into this contradictory character who casts himself first as the aggrieved husband and then as the noble rescuer of a foolish and erring wife – and who finally must seek to be as good a man as he has imagined himself to be all along. Lewis's screenplay fantasies are a melodrama of his own devising, and in the genuinely disturbing events that overtake him and Elizabeth, the film puts Lewis to a test. Life and art, even pulp art, are not so easily distinguished as Lewis may have supposed. Fictions, however extreme, the film seems to say, are in fact the stuff of life and one's only (or necessary) way of making sense of it.

The three different visualizations of Lewis's script (all accompanied by lush romantic music) are preceded by shots of him composing at the typewriter in his study, listening to music through earphones while he struggles to write scenes between Elizabeth and her supposed lover. In the first (presumably in Lewis's imagined version of Baden-Baden since the city's tour book lies next to his typewriter), Elizabeth and Hursa (whose back is to the camera because Lewis has yet to meet the young poet) are in a cafe outside whose window is a terrace of empty chairs and tables. Elizabeth confides her innermost thoughts about needing to get away from everyone ("even from the child I love") in order to find herself. The gloomy weather matches the pseudomelancholic mood in which she earnestly and pretentiously delivers the sentimental, confessional drivel that Lewis delights in having her mouth. Lewis even ascribes to her the ideological slogan earlier spoken by Isabel – "Women are an occupied country." The moment this line is delivered, however, Lewis's comically spiteful imagination envisions a large red truck in the far background turning in the direction of the couple. As Elizabeth delivers her final line to the silent Hursa, "I know you will understand because you are a poet," the speeding truck smashes through the terrace chairs and tables, bearing down on the couple. Even Lewis cannot let this jealous and hilariously vengeful scene stand, and the next shot shows him tossing out the page he has been writing.

The second episode occurs after Hursa has spent some time living with the Fieldings in England. It depicts, in stilted, symmetrically posed profile, a nude Elizabeth and Hursa conversing at a Baden-Baden spa (Figure 41). Elizabeth tells a rapt Hursa about her writer-husband and of the couple's travels in the days when they were freer, before the birth of their son. This episode ends on Elizabeth's line to Hursa, "I would love to hear one of your poems." The next shot is not of Lewis in his study as before, but of the gazebo where Elizabeth is gardening and Hursa typing invitations to a party Elizabeth has perversely decided to give for "all the people we don't know." Elizabeth looks up to say, "I'd love to hear one of your poems." Whereas Lewis has freely incorporated lines from daily conversation into his script, it now seems that the script is providing lines for Elizabeth. Such interpenetration of Lewis's script and the framing narration also characterizes the third of Lewis's screenplay scenes, which depicts Elizabeth and Hursa dancing in the restaurant where they later dine just before running off together. Moreover, her conversation in this scene seems incongruous in two respects: she dances intimately with Hursa while expressing her anxiety over her responsibilities as a mother, and her dialogue seems an exaggerated extension of an actual conversation she had with Hursa earlier, which Lewis was not privy to and thus could hardly expand on. Such permeability raises questions about the levels of narration in the discourse. At one level, all of these scenes are explainable as Lewis's subjective visualizations of his script. Certainly his jealousy and oft-stated suspicions (to say nothing of his writer's ego) are evident, but is the overall style of such scenes solely ascribable to Lewis? The overwrought acting, the mock solemnity, and the too perfect symmetry of the compositions signal parody in each episode, and a dimension of the excess seems to belong not just to Lewis but to the third-person narration as well. Lewis the writer of pulp fiction is mocked as surely as he mocks his characters. Even more suggestively, the dialogue in his script that echoes and anticipates dialogue in scenes of which he can have no knowledge points to more than his character-narration. The film's overall third-person narration suggests a reciprocity whose irony embraces Lewis and sees that he gets what he has imagined.

A more perplexing question of narrational origin centers on a later repetition of the lift scene. In a darkened bedroom the camera moves over the figure of Lewis and continues until it frames only Elizabeth in the same bed in a close-up of her face and open eyes; one hears discordant music that signals the cut to the now familiar lift scene, which was previously linked to Lewis and his jealous fantasy. A suggestive ambiguity arises from the clash of narrational conventions. What has been in the past (and perhaps still is) Lewis's mindscreen, now seems Elizabeth's. The sound associated with the lift is not heard until after Lewis is excluded from the frame by the track to Elizabeth and close-up of her face. On the strength of past associations this instance of the lift scene would seem to belong to Lewis; however, both the sound track and the preceding shot of Elizabeth now suggest otherwise. Has Lewis's fantasy somehow been transferred, passed on to Elizabeth as is later the case when she confirms his fears by running away with Thomas? Or is this scene Elizabeth's memory of what actually happened in the lift in Baden-Baden, or perhaps her own sexual fantasy that anticipates the seduction yet to happen in the gazebo? Is the fantasy somehow "shared" by both of them, or perhaps ascribable to the third-person narration? There are no definitive answers to these questions. Nor do the ambiguities stop here, for the lift scene is followed by a return to the bedroom, where Lewis begins to make love to Elizabeth. If Lewis's amorous actions are somehow motivated by the fantasy, does it not necessarily place the lift fantasy in his mind once again?

The narrational issues are made only more problematic when the final instance of the lift shots is interpolated into the actual seduction scene in the gazebo. Here, briefly, is a description of five successive shots: (1) a high-angle shot of the lovers in the gazebo; (2) a direct overhead shot of the descending lift, previously seen in the Baden-Baden episode, but never a part of Lewis's fantasy; (3) a medium close-up of Elizabeth's face during the gazebo seduction; (4) an extremely brief shot of her face at a nearly identical moment in the lift scene; (5) a shot of the lovers in the gazebo that zooms back to a high-angle long shot. The direct overhead shot of the descending lift apparently belongs to the third-person narration, although that is not certain. Impossible to decipher, the shot conveys a sense of falling, of vertigo, of loss of control that might well represent Elizabeth's sexuality either through third-person narration or mindscreen. The brief fourth shot, similar to those in Lewis's fantasy, may be Elizabeth's mindscreen and/or part of the omniscient narration. Does the film grant access to Elizabeth's mind, to her subjective thoughts, through this shot and perhaps the earlier lift scene intercut with the couple in bed? Possibly, but there are no other such instances anywhere in the discourse. If so, however, the later lift scenes provide brief but significant internal access to Elizabeth's character and prepare for, though not explain, her action in running off with Thomas Hursa. Whatever the answer, and none is certain, the narrational ambiguity itself becomes a metaphor for Elizabeth's finally subscribing to and enacting the basic fantasy with which Lewis has tormented her and himself. More comprehensively, the ambiguity addresses a central theme in the film that is also an issue in Wiseman's novel – the struggle of the storyteller to tell a story or, more accurately, the struggle among the various storytellers (Lewis the scriptwriter, Lewis the husband, Elizabeth the wife, Elizabeth the "scripted" character, Hursa the drug dealer/gigolo, Hursa the critic of the bourgoisie, and even the omniscient narrator of the discourse) to tell their stories.

In many ways *The Romantic Englishwoman* is one of Losey's more overtly ideological films in that he and Stoppard foreground both the Fieldings' comfortable bourgeois ways and an ongoing critique of their life (Figure 38). Thomas is, of course, the catalyst for this indictment, which Lewis and Elizabeth seem to bring on themselves. When on Hursa's first evening in Weybridge Elizabeth attacks him for taking advantage of people, for the irresponsible way he has of letting others look after him, she is baffled by his reply: "It takes some of the burden off them." Interestingly, Lewis is the one who elaborates on Hursa's cryptic remark by saying: "He means that owners are under the pressure of ownership, the strain of hanging on to everything. Houses. Jobs. Wives... Fools, in fact... Because all the time we are locking the doors and setting up the burglar alarms, watching over the loved ones, we are being robbed of our lives, the full expression of our lives." Although Lewis somewhat disarmingly makes Hursa's argument, his knowing tone seems meant simultaneously to express and undercut the relevance of such observations. Lewis's articulation of the paradoxes of bourgeois life ends with the following exchange with Elizabeth:

ELIZABETH: Yes, but you don't live like that.
LEWIS: No. I live with the burden of possession.
ELIZABETH: Possessiveness!
LEWIS: Desire. Love.

The pattern here is clear, for what starts as an attack on Hursa's ingratiating ways of taking advantage of the rich ends with the Fieldings' struggle to understand each other and the mutual suspicions that characterize their bourgeois life. Possessiveness, desire, and love are not casually chosen terms, for they define the contentions surrounding their marriage. That Lewis would list wives among the possessions that need guarding suggests how thoroughly bourgeois materialism may corrupt personal relations. Elizabeth struggles under the threat of just such objectification, which gives weight to her charge of possessiveness against Lewis. That Lewis should counter her charge with his own terms, desire and love, is equally revealing. Much of the time Lewis is obsessed less with his own desire than with the possibility, the threat, of Elizabeth enacting hers. Lewis's fantasies, both involuntary and willed, and the narrational complexities of *The Romantic Englishwoman* point to the centrality of these issues. Whether their relationship moves from possessiveness through desire to love is a question raised by the concluding scenes as Elizabeth's impulsive running off with Hursa leads eventually to Lewis's "rescue" of her.

The various, even competing attitudes and concerns of *The Romantic Englishwoman* finally coalesce around the character and narrative function of Hursa, whose drug-smuggling activities are the film's invention rather than Wiseman's. The result is an audacious mix in which Losey shrewdly plays off the assumptions and patterns of one genre against another, which makes for a good deal of witty irony, particularly in the Fieldings' misunderstanding of the reasons for Thomas's presence. For them Thomas is a strange and provocative intruder into their marital conflict, in other words a character in their story, subordinate to their needs and claims. But for Thomas, Lewis and Elizabeth are merely an episode in the thriller that has been his story, as it were, all along. Were Hursa only the gigolo-intruder the Fieldings believe him to be, a satire of social values and contemporary marriage would be the film's only subject. His status as a smuggler on the run, however, is something of a wild card. The implications of the thriller genre, which were introduced in the Baden-Baden segment and have lain dormant for much of the time since then, reappear and considerably complicate the film's concluding section. The flight of Elizabeth and Thomas is the most problematic element of the film, and the most daring. The tensions between the different genre elements assume an emotional and moral intensity that is darker and much less easily resolved than one might have expected from the wit (even savage wit) and cleverness that have gone before.

As a character Elizabeth is subjected to enormous pressure by the story's events and, in a different sense, by the expectations of the renewed thriller pattern. If adventure fascinates her, it is the least likely of modes to fulfill Elizabeth, and yet an adventure, in which she is pushed steadily to the margin, is mostly what she is confined to. Moreover, she embraces its promise of escape more than the genuine freedom she has so often spoken of. Indeed, Isabel, in a scene sharply contrasting with their earlier confrontation, tells Lewis: "Elizabeth hasn't got what it takes to be free the way she wants . . . For Elizabeth, Thomas is freedom, and that makes it sexy. People make too much of sex. It shouldn't be anything you leave home for." However facile Isabel's judgments, they are telling. Lewis counters with no more than token objections; he is bereft, which is all the more obvious for his being surrounded by the photographs of the absent Elizabeth. If Elizabeth's need to escape Lewis's game playing and controlling jealousy is understandable, her actions are nonetheless futile. Her whispered voice-over, "my poet," which accompanies the long shot of the couple's car as they drive through southern Europe, is most problematic. Her invocation to romance with "my poet" is doubly ironic, for Thomas is not one to be possessed, and his status as a poet, or as a character she understands in any depth, is certainly in question. At night she hovers watchfully over the sleeping Thomas, unable to sleep herself, seemingly suspended between her amazement at being there and her anxiety that her poet may disappear. She seems no less defined by Thomas now than by Lewis before him. Having run away from Lewis and their son and all the anxieties she felt as a mother, she is left to a kind of child's game (literally playing "jacks" at the seaside) without responsibilities and obligations, but also without purpose. That Elizabeth and Thomas should run away together for quite different purposes, rooted not just in their individual characters but in the underlying genres to which each in a sense belongs, reflects the film's command of its disparate tones and elements. Thomas's purpose is eminently practical: he has been discovered by an associate of his mysterious pursuer and must flee for his life. Elizabeth seems only to have accepted Lewis's fantasy that Thomas will be her lover.

To his credit, Thomas never lies to Elizabeth. When he learns that she has left home without any money, stocks, or even jewelry, he is dismayed. Ruefully calling her a "crazy woman," he begins to understand the extent of her naively romantic illusions and how unprepared she is for the life she thinks she has chosen. Unconcerned about money, she tells Thomas they can live as he has lived in the past. He tells her the truth: he has always lived for himself and would not make her happy. In a curiously touching scene when they are in bed together, Thomas tells Elizabeth about the way he has lived, about "those romantic ladies" he could easily please and who took nothing from him. He has spoken of this much earlier, but always lightly, without feeling. Now, however, he speaks with intensity. To Elizabeth's fearful question, "I'm not one of them, am I?" he replies, "The Englishwoman was the most romantic. All she wanted was everything." The disarmingly self-centered adventurer is quite gentle in his attempt to make Elizabeth see the reality so at odds with her dream of romance, and he urges her to return home. In their last scenes together, the poet and the romantic Englishwoman sit quietly by the sea. He gives her a small bouquet of flowers; he strokes her hair and wordlessly makes his farewell. The next day he has found himself another wealthy older woman.

Elizabeth is not free but rather a refugee from her life, a condition that is echoed reflexively in her status as a character with no place of her own in the thriller genre that dominates the last section of the film. When Lewis arrives, she learns that Thomas phoned him to come for her. Perhaps Thomas's philosophy is anarchic, as Losey said, but the measure of his character, the quality that makes him more than just an adventurer or a catalyst in the struggle between Lewis and Elizabeth, is the moral responsibility he accepts at the end. Thomas is not redeemed by his actions, but he is revealed as more complex than either Lewis or Elizabeth (or perhaps the viewer) has supposed. That Lewis, despite his effort to prevent it, has led the gangsters to Thomas results in an irony more poignant than bitter. "What should I do?" asks Lewis as he watches Thomas being abducted. Thomas's seemingly flippant reply, "Get a new secretary," both relieves Lewis of the responsibility of interfering and concludes the thriller story. What remains is Lewis's reunion with Elizabeth.

Does Lewis transcend his obsessive jealousy or merely enact the rescue of a woman who "finds herself out of her depth," as he once described the wife in his screenplay? His concluding declaration of care, protectiveness, and love for her seems genuine:

ELIZABETH: Why have you come?
LEWIS: I've come to take you home.

ELIZABETH: Why?

LEWIS: I love you.

ELIZABETH: Why do you?

LEWIS: He phoned me and told me where to come. I don't want you to come to harm.

ELIZABETH: No.

Although his sentiments can be understood as more patronizing or paternalistic than loving, Lewis's feelings appear direct and revelatory of what he has come to understand about himself and the dangers of his game playing. And one senses that Elizabeth asks her questions not out of shame or guilt, but out of a guarded yet insistent need to know what lies behind his declaration of love. The film does not simply indict Elizabeth for acting out her desire or for searching for an identity beyond her bourgeois home. Nor does it endorse Lewis's obsessive jealousy, manipulativeness, and drive for control. Instead, *The Romantic Englishwoman* explores their mutually destructive attitudes and actions, never settling for a too simple social criticism or merely an exposé of bourgeois values. Once again Losey has made a "picture of provocation" in which social and moral issues, however prominent, are embedded in the complexities and contradictions of character rather than only emblemized by them. One need only recall the conclusions to the Losey–Pinter films to recognize the efficacy of the ending to this film. Barrett, having usurped the world of the aristocratic Tony, locks up the town house as *The Servant* ends. But his act entraps the inhabitants as effectively as it locks out any outsiders. In *Accident* Stephen retrieves his children from outside and returns to the house as the sound of the accident that killed William is repeated on the sound track. The sound and the image of the placid facade of Stephen's house, which replicate the film's opening shot, now belie the moral corruption that forever holds Stephen's present captive to his past. In the last image of *The Go-Between,* the car in which the older Leo Colston rides stops at the now abandoned and ruined Brandham Hall, an apt symbol of Leo's empty, unlived life. Entrapment, hypocrisy, victimization, betrayal of self, violence, and desolation are among the rewards of those who through social class, sexual manipulation, and deception seek to control others. The final image of *The Romantic Englishwoman* that shows Elizabeth sitting in silent desolation beside Lewis in a car outside their house hardly presages a happy future (Figure 42). If Thomas, the intruder, is gone, the Fieldings are still held hostage by their bourgeois life. Both shut in and shut out, the Fieldings can see and hear from their car the revelry of the forgotten but invited party guests who now occupy their house.

In general, the world of Losey's films is not a hospitable one for women. In some films and for some women characters, this inhospitality is a key issue that is directly addressed and explored. The restrictions of class and the constrictions of contemporary marriage can serve to imprison them; Marian Maudsley and Elizabeth Fielding are both caught in socially conventional roles against which they struggle but from which they fail to escape. In other films the women, due to a deliberate emphasis on their supposedly enigmatic quality (or perhaps, occasionally, to peculiarities in the script), are underdeveloped or incomplete characters; Vera in *The Servant* and Anna in *Accident*, for instance, function primarily as objects of the sexual obsessions of the male characters. However central to the plot, these two women reside near the margins of their respective stories. *The Servant*, like much of Losey's work, centers on male protagonists and their complex, frequently competitive relationships with other men; *King and Country, Accident, Figures in a Landscape, The Assassination of Trotsky* (1972), and *Mr. Klein* are further examples. Susan, in *The Servant*, is an inconsistent character whose subservience toward Barrett in the end seems inexplicable in light of her earlier assertive, even combative, stance against him. Ultimately, she is banished, the outsider who can only witness the symbiotic, destructive relationship between the two men.

It distorts the Losey canon, however, to see his work as solely male-dominated. His last two films, *La Truite* and *Steaming*, continue to explore women characters and issues that Losey had addressed as early as *Eve* and as late as *A Doll's House* (1973) and *The Romantic Englishwoman*. The young heroine of *La Truite*, Frédérique (Isabelle Huppert), is in many ways Elizabeth Fielding's opposite. Elizabeth struggles to have a life and a story outside of the controlling power of her screenwriter husband. Her "romantic" projections onto Hursa, whom she calls in whispered voice-over "my poet," suggest how short-lived her escape will be. Frédérique, in contrast, is in control and even protective of her homosexual, alcoholic husband, Galuchat, just as her marriage to him offers a first line of defense against other, predatory men. She can go off to Japan with another man who hopes in vain to be her lover. Like Anna in *Accident*, she can be the tabula rasa onto which the men project their sexual fantasies, but unlike Anna, Frédérique controls her situation. Aware of the libidinous men surrounding her, she determines never to be a victim. Her power resides in the space between "peut-être" (perhaps) and "jamais" (never), the contradictory word-signs that appear respectively on the front and back of her shirt. Frédérique's sexual unavailability, unlike Elizabeth's desire, empowers her; ultimately, through this sexual invulnerability, she establishes absolute control, social and economic, over the competitive, obsessive men in the world of multi-national corporations where she flourishes. Her final line in the film – "Galuchat does everything" – is both deeply dismissive of the business world and an ironic comment about the supposed power of the businessmen she now controls.

In several ways, Losey's last film is unlike anything he did before. The all-male casts of *King and Country* and *Figures in a Landscape* find their counterpart in the exclusively female cast of *Steaming*. The film is built around the personal and political bonding of women who take common action to fight the closing and proposed destruction of their community bathhouse. To be sure, class conflicts arise between Nancy (Vanessa Redgrave), the wealthy housewife, and Josie (Patti Love), the working-class woman whose language and accent keep her unemployed. That Nancy has been abandoned by her husband and Josie physically abused by her lover point to experiences that bridge their class differences. The bathhouse is a haven or sanctuary for the women, and their "steaming" is in anger over the inequities of a sexist society. If the characters first seem little more than conventional types engaged in polemics, they gradually become more in-dividualized. And if didacticism threatens the film, leavening is found in the fine performances, particularly of Sarah Miles and Vanessa Redgrave, and in the happy, even celebratory, ending described by screenwriter Patricia Losey as "a message of hope . . . based on human contact" (Ciment 1985, 386). These words express sentiments appropriate to Losey's first films – *The Boy with Green Hair* and *The Lawless*. With *Steaming*, his career comes full circle.

Losey's interest in women's experience and issues in these films is, of course, no guarantee of a depth or breadth of understanding. Indeed, the feminist content of two of his films comes directly out of the stageplays, Ibsen's *A Doll's House* and Nell Dunn's *Steaming*, from which they were adapted. Speaking of *Steaming*, Patricia Losey notes that "the film is about women, a subject of perplexity for Joe" (Ciment 1985, 386). Still, Losey struggled throughout his career to understand the dynamics between men and women, and his interests, attitudes, and focus changed over the years. But as different as *The Romantic Englishwoman*, *La Truite*, and *Steaming* are, they are recognizably Losey films, no less compassionate toward their characters than they are sensitive to injustice and hypocrisy. Whether in marriage, the business world, or the public bathhouse, questions of equity and justice arise at the point where sex, power, and politics converge.

7
"No Ready-Made Answers"

A baroque stylist, a formalist filmmaker more involved in exploring elaborate settings or experimenting with cinematic time than in caring about his characters; a pessimistic allegorist who paints, then damns, the darkness; or a humanist, generous and compassionate, attuned to the injustice of racial and class prejudice, and an enemy of hypocrites and opportunists – such labeling, a makeup of truths and half-truths, of distortions, misconceptions, and some insight as well, obscures a full and thoughtful view of Joseph Losey, who abhorred labeling of any kind. Beginning as a director of films posing answers to social problems, he became a director compelled by emotional and moral dilemmas lacking ready answers. Cautious about making "heroes where there are no heroes and villains where there are no villains," Losey said that "I incline, and always have, to the thought that it's pretty hard to find absolute good and absolute evil in any one person. But of the existence of good and evil I have no doubt" (Gow 1971, 37).

A controversial and uncompromising artist, Losey was aware that his films placed certain demands on the viewer. "I don't want to do anyone's thinking for them," he said.

> Instead, I wish to give people the benefit of my particular observations, of my particular eye, my particular view of things, and also of such passion as I feel about various things. Sometimes my view is highly passionate, and sometimes it's highly destructive rather than constructive, but I have no ready-made statements, no ready-made answers, no easy emotional identifications. (1970, 59)

One can imagine, however, Losey endorsing Thomas Hardy's sentiment – "If a way to the better there be, it lies in taking a full look at the worst." A hard look at characters in moral crisis, characters who often stumble by failing to act on their better instincts and end by betraying themselves as well as others – such is the treacherous ground his characters walk. But, importantly, in his finest films Losey's sensibility as an artist is drawn not simply to issues of moral choice or to the risk of failure, but to the particular ways individual people live with both. Defeat and loss are common in his films, but so, too, are what he called "internal rewards," the possibilities of moral growth, commitment, and even love where the forces arrayed against such values might seem too powerful to permit them any place at all.

Losey's films leave open many questions because the world invoked in them is an uncertain, enclosed, ambiguous one where characters can be overwhelmed by evil from without and from within. In the early films (*The Boy with Green Hair*, *The Lawless*, and *M* [1951], his American remake of Fritz Lang's German masterpiece), the conformity of a mob and its potential for violence are indicted, but as his work matured, Losey turned his attention to subtle and incisive character studies. His characters are placed in very particularized and detailed environments. The British army, Oxford, the world of the aristocracy – each has its own complex structures and injustices; the films insist, nevertheless, on accountability, on personal responsibility. Social systems can be inhumane – and Losey's films indict them – but they are so because people choose to act cowardly, hypocritically, cruelly. There are other choices available to people, to Losey's characters, and the choices are not mere abstractions or emblems of some ideal. If the motivations of his characters often remain unclear, their actions and the decisions they make have real human consequences.

The films analyzed in this book depict some characters rationalizing and evading responsibility; the colonel in *King and Country*, Tony and Barrett in *The Servant*, Marian and Mrs. Maudsley in *The Go-Between* are all examples. There are others who are victims – Hamp and Hargreaves and Leo Colston. Still others like Stephen in *Accident* struggle and fail; or continue to struggle – Lewis and perhaps Elizabeth in *The Romantic Englishwoman* ultimately come to accept and understand the costs of their actions. Surely, Hargreaves and Hamp have their illusions in place at the beginning of *King and Country*; Hargreaves thinks that he knows himself and what to do with deserters. Hamp knows that the British army cannot kill him because he has survived the worst already in his three years at the front. Both Lewis and Elizabeth confront their respective illusions about control and escape as the scripted world of one and the romantic escapade of the other conflate and collapse. The goal of most of Losey's characters, though they would hardly be aware of it or want to pursue it, is disillusionment.

Tony and Barrett, Stephen and Charley, Leo, and the Fieldings – all are the victims in different ways, and admittedly for different reasons, of elaborate game playing. At stake more often than not are power and sex, for power and sex and how they are substituted one for the other describe the dynamics, the maneuvers, and shifting alignments of the characters whose capacity for deceit also harbors self-deception. To be disabused of self-deception, of delusions (or in Tony's case to surrender completely to them), accounts for the desolation that marks their end. In the conclusions to these films, the characters may be consigned to defeat, a moral defeat for some – surely for Tony and Barrett, and for the unknowing Marian and the all too self-knowing Stephen. But defeat for Hargreaves and for Leo (even, modestly, for Lewis) is tempered, perhaps even transcended, through a reckoning with conscience and a deepening recognition of loss, guilt, and grief.

What can make Losey's films seem especially difficult is that his aesthetic strategies and structural complexities sometimes initially create a distance between his characters and the audience. As he has said, there are "no easy emotional identifications" in his films. The intricate handling of time and the layered narrational structures in his films provide intellectual challenge; Losey himself spoke more than once of his fascination with the resources of his medium, and there was a measure of the intellectual in that fascination. But the greater importance of his exploration of those resources was grounded in his mature rejection of ready-made statements and answers, which are inevitably implied by the structured causality and apparently seamless dramatic logic of classical narration and narrative. Losey shared with his finest collaborator, Harold Pinter, the conviction that "life is much more mysterious than plays [and films] make it out to be"; in the mode of art cinema they sought to allow for mystery, to render the real experience of time as people live it rather than as the simple linear chain that classical narrative depends upon. Almost paradoxically, the underlying functions of Losey's experimentation with form are primarily moral and emotional ones. The character-narrations in *Accident* and *The Go-Between* simultaneously provide the time-past world and the character's subjective experience and assessment of it, just as the character-narrations in *The Romantic Englishwoman* convey the fears and overripe fantasies of the Fieldings. Losey uses the resources of cinema, then, to present the inner life of his characters, to convey another kind of realism, another way that people live in and experience the world. With such films he risked much, for he knew as surely as T. S. Eliot that "... human kind / Cannot bear very much reality. / Time past and time future / What might have been and what has been / Point to one end, which is the present."

Notes

Chapter 1

1. In his forthcoming biography of Losey, British author David Caute draws on the filmmaker's personal papers, which were bequeathed to the British Film Institute. With its publication in early 1993, Caute's biography will certainly become the standard reference for the details of Losey's life.

2. In the film's American release, under the title *Finger of Guilt,* the director's credit was given to Alec Snowden, who was the producer, rather than "Joseph Walton," Losey's pseudonym.

3. Various terms have been applied to these aspects. This book will follow the usage in Seymour Chatman's *Story and Discourse: Narrative Structure in Fiction and Film.* Chatman defines *story* as "events and existents (characters and setting)" and *discourse* as "the means through which the story is transmitted" (1978, 9). David Bordwell, drawing on the Russian formalist tradition, prefers "*fabula* (sometimes translated as 'story')...[which] embodies the action as a chronological, cause-and-effect chain of events occurring within a given duration and spatial field," and "*syuzhet* (usually translated as 'plot')...[which is] the actual arrangement and presentation of the fabula in the film" (1985, 49–50).

4. Despite a brilliant screenplay, which Losey thought "the absolute height of [Pinter's] accomplishment" and the American critic Stanley Kauffmann judged the finest adaptation of a major work he had ever read, Losey and Pinter were never able to obtain the necessary financing to produce the film. Eventually, in an unusual move, *The Proust Screenplay* was published in 1977.

5. Ironically, despite its status as a defining element of narrative, whatever the medium, narration in film received little attention until such studies as Bruce Kawin's *Mindscreen* (1978), which deals with filmic first person, a section of articles on "point of view" in *Film Reader 4* (1979), and Nick Browne's *The Rhetoric of Filmic Narration* (1982) demonstrated narration's centrality to an understanding of film narrative. The publication in English of *Narrative Discourse: An Essay in Method* (1980) by French literary theorist Gerard Genette provided an additional, major impetus for the study of what has come to be known as narratology. Soon after, Brian Henderson's "Tense, Mood, and Voice in Film: Notes after Genette" (1983)

imported and tested some of Genette's ideas in the realm of film theory. Edward R. Branigan's *Point of View in the Cinema* (1984), David Bordwell's *Narration in the Fiction Film* (1985), a special issue of the journal *Wide Angle* (vol. 8, nos. 3–4, 1986), and Sarah Kozloff's *Invisible Storytellers* (1988) widened the discussion further. While Genette's views – notably his notion of multiple levels of narration and narrative – are not controlling in all of these studies, they hover influentially behind many of the arguments.

6. Among the disputed (and fundamental) contentions in film theories of narration is that which rejects traditional literary notions, preferring to treat filmic narration as a process not dependent on a narrator. Branigan asserts that " 'narrator' is a metaphor, an anthropomorphism," contending that narration "is not a person or a state of mind, but a linguistic and logical relationship posed by the text as a condition of its intelligibility" (1984, 3). Similarly, David Bordwell argues that "to give every film a narrator or implied author is to indulge in an anthropomorphic fiction" (1985, 62). And George M. Wilson states that "there are no grounds for recognizing in narrative film a being, personlike or not, who fictionally offers our view of narrative events to us" (1986, 135). (Interestingly, these and other writers who would jettison a narrator from film as an unsupportable fiction frequently have recourse to the term "narrator," nonetheless.) Such views come close to substituting one kind of anthropomorphism for another. Carried to its extreme, this proposition leads to David Alan Black's assertion that the first-level narration in film "belongs to the medium itself" (1986, 22). By contrast, in a review of Bordwell's book Chatman counters that the claim that film narration "presupposes a perceiver, but not any sender, of a message" is semiotically impossible, and maintains that it is "a mistake to reject the cinematic narrator" (1986, 140). So, too, in her review of Bordwell's book Sarah Kozloff observes: "How can a message be deliberately organized for a perceiver but not have any sender? How can stories, in any moment of history, tell themselves? Bordwell condemns the positing of a grand image-maker as an 'anthropomorphic fiction' and goes on to transfer...human activities and qualities to an abstract process" (1986, 44).

7. In *Mindscreen* Kawin maintains that the fundamental test of narrating voice resides in a narrative's overall logic. In other words, whom does the logic of the discourse present (either explicitly or implicitly) as narrating? Kawin argues that filmic narration is not confined to the third person, but rather possesses the capacity for a sustained first-person voice as well. In his view, which is not inconsistent with Genette's, a discursive presentation of the "field of the mind's eye," what a character thinks (e.g., memories, dreams, and fantasies), constitutes a form of first-person or character-narration, which Kawin calls "mindscreen," that may be embedded in a larger third-person discourse or may encompass an entire narrative. In a later article, "An Outline of Film Voices," Kawin maintains the necessity "to establish whether deliberate, personalized narration is taking place, whether a given view is objective or subjective, whether whatever subjectivity does appear is authorial" (1984–5, 39). The issue of subjectivity, which both Kawin and Branigan emphasize, is crucial, for, as this book will argue, Losey's films with Pinter and Stoppard extend the realm of subjectivity well beyond the limits of classical narration.

8. See Bordwell (1985, 205–33). Distinguishing art-cinema narration from classical narration (defined by traditional Hollywood studio filmmaking), Bordwell identifies

three "interlocking procedural schemata – 'objective' realism, 'expressive' or subjective realism, and narrational commentary." The first of these, 'objective' realism, deemphasizes the structured drama of classical narration, "seeking to depict the vagaries of real life." The second, 'expressive' or subjective realism, seeks to render an inner reality, emphasizing a character's subjective experience of events rather than the events themselves. The third, narrational commentary, differs from the norms of classical narration by highlighting the narrational act as "an intermittently present but highly noticeable external authority through which we gain access to [the story]."

Chapter 2

1. In *The Great War and Modern Memory* Paul Fussell observes: "No one was to know too much. Until 1916, the parents of soldiers executed for 'acts prejudicial to military discipline' were given the news straight, but after agitation by Sylvia Pankhurst, they were informed by telegram that their soldier had 'died of wounds' " (1977, 176). Fussell's brilliant cultural history of the war contains many passages that provide illuminating commentary on issues raised in Losey's film. The book includes chapters on war as ironic action, on life in the trenches, on mythic and ritual patterns, and on the sexual (homoerotic) nature of front-line experience.
2. Reflecting on his use of these images, Losey told Ciment, "Those early flashes of stills at the beginning of *King and Country* [are] partly the stirrings of *Accident*, of *The Go-Between*, of *Proust*" (1985, 244).
3. Unless otherwise noted, all quotations of dialogue from the films are taken directly from their sound tracks. In an unexplained departure from Housman's text, the lines from poem "XXXVI" in *More Poems* (1936) are changed. Housman wrote:

> Here dead lie we because we did not choose
>   To live and shame the land from which we sprung.
> Life, to be sure, is nothing much to lose;
>   But young men think it is, and we were young.

4. These issues are also raised by a different kind of story contained *within* the omniscient narration but not, strictly speaking, produced by a character-narrator: first, the formal charge read at the court-martial and then, at the end of the film, the telegram from the War Office to Hamp's survivors. (The telegram is read in voice-over by Dirk Bogarde, who is not speaking in the character of Captain Hargreaves.) Each of these is a kind of mini discourse from which a story of Hamp's actions is intended to be inferred by those to whom it is addressed. These two "official stories," of course, flatly contradict each other. In the charge Hamp is a deserter, and for this he will be shot. In the telegram he is a soldier who was "killed in action," and the "deep regret" expressed is presumably on behalf of his king and country.
5. This scene ends with Hargreaves quoting a line from Lewis Carroll's *Alice's Adventures in Wonderland* ("There's a porpoise close behind me, and he's treading on my tail"), which he then punctuates with the single word "Facts." The colonel has the last word, however, answering Hargreaves with the rueful lines from John Masefield's long poem "Biography":

When I am buried, and all my thoughts and acts
Will be reduced to lists of dates and facts,
And long before this wandering flesh is rotten
The dates which made me will be all forgotten.

In its way, this odd exchange points to what Paul Fussell calls "the unparalleled literariness" of the war and to the great disparities that existed between the officers and men, which was emphasized, he wrote, "not merely by separate quarters and messes and different uniforms and weapons but by different accents and diction and syntaxes and allusions" (1977, 82).

Chapter 3

1. Losey and Pinter disagreed in their recollections about the original screenplay and its relationship to the actual shooting script. In "The Losey–Pinter Collaboration" Beverle Houston and Marsha Kinder quote the following remarks: "Losey: 'Our finished film uses about one-fifth or a quarter of the original Pinter script written before I came into it.' Pinter: 'I must make it quite clear that I didn't write a second script. I modified and developed to a certain extent the first script' " (1978, 17–18).
2. Losey ascribed this uncertainty to casting, calling Susan's social status "very obscure in the film." He told Milne, "I like Wendy Craig as an actress enormously, I like her personally, and after much searching I gave her the part. When we began shooting, I asked her to try to assume an upper-class manner and accent; and it was utterly hopeless.... Ideally that girl should have been entirely believable as of upper-class background" (1968, 141).

Chapter 4

1. Edward Branigan argues that "simultaneous with character narration there is always present an underlying omniscient, third person narration, which creates the fictional appearance of other narrations or levels within the text" (1984, 41). Bruce Kawin takes a different view, accepting the *possibility* of an underlying level (particularly of authorial comment) but not its necessity. Bordwell aptly observes that "within the art cinema's mode of production and reception, the concept of the author has a formal function it did not possess in the Hollywood studio system." Among other factors, he notes, "director's statements of intent guide the comprehension of the film, while a body of work linked by an authorial signature encourages viewers to read each film as a chapter of an oeuvre. Thus the institutional 'author' is available as a source of the formal operation of the film" (1985, 211). In effect, the director of art cinema, who is equated with the author of literary texts, is a source precisely because there is a larger body of his work to which the individual film can be referred. (This seems equally true of such Hollywood filmmakers as John Ford or Alfred Hitchcock.) But are authorial comment and narrational commentary the same thing? Bordwell seems to elide the distinction between author and narrator – in part, no doubt, because he favors a view of narration as a process or system. By contrast, this book will maintain that just as the author and narrator of Pudovkin's *Mother* or Truffaut's *The 400 Blows* (for all the latter's autobiographical associa-

tions), like those of Hemingway's *The Sun Also Rises,* remain distinct, so do those of the author(s) of *Accident, The Go-Between,* or *The Romantic Englishwoman* and the films' narrators.

2. In discussing what he terms "character reflection and projection," Branigan says that they "occur in (1) present time and depend on a (2) *metaphorical framing* [emphasis added] which links the character to the production of space, as opposed to a framing which is literally from the character's point in space, such as a point of view shot.... The objects are linked to character by a narrative inference and their presentation is (supposedly) modulated by a particular kind of character attention – normal awareness, fear, guilt, desire, etc." (1984, 123). The significance of "narrative inference" is reminiscent of Kawin's view that the test of voice resides in a narrative's overall logic.

3. Houston and Kinder conclude that although *Accident* "does not use conventional first-person techniques, we see things primarily through Stephen's point of view, which is established by the flashback structure; but we don't have access to his thoughts and motives" (1978, 21). The question of character point of view is related to Kawin's argument in "An Outline of Film Voices," particularly his reconsideration of a narrating voice anchored in the perspective of a single character. In *Mindscreen* Kawin identified a single category labeled "point of view" and treated as a variant of the third person, a voice that "subjectivized the world but not the narrative" (1978, 18). In "Outline" he moves this mode to first person, calling attention to its *apparent* objectivity while distinguishing it from a newly defined mode called "perspectival presentation," a third-person voice of "implied authorial perspective on what is shown" (1984–5, 41 and 44).

4. Focusing on the addressee, Branigan observes in a similar context that the "*voyeuristic* reader is the unseen and unacknowledged spectator for whom an address is, apparently, unaddressed (to no one); that is, the text does not acknowledge its viewer" (1984, 44).

5. Within the overall omniscient narration Neff dictates a recording to his boss in which he narrates the story of his relationship with Phyllis Dietrichson, the murder of her husband, and his own subsequent betrayal by her. Thus, Neff's narration has an intended addressee in the discourse; the audience can be said to eavesdrop on his narrative. Stevenson's *Jane Eyre* opens with a shot of what is ostensibly the book from which the film is adapted and returns to highlighted pages at intervals throughout the discourse. In voice-over the title character begins by reading the words on a lighted page: "My name is Jane Eyre." This and other passages similarly presented are not from the novel, however, but from a voice-over narration written for the film. Interestingly, the film posits via the images of the book and its pages an overall first-person narrator. In *Invisible Storytellers* Sarah Kozloff agrees with those critics who believe that "behind the voice-over narrator there is another presence that supplements the nominal narrator's vision, knowledge, and storytelling powers." She points out, however, that "in many cases the voice-over narrator is so inscribed in the film as to seem as if he or she has generated not only what he is saying but also what we are seeing.... The single most crucial factor in our acceptance of the pose is that the film emphasize the character's claim to be telling the story" (1988, 44–5). Jane's narration, like Neff's, has an addressee; it is, however, neither herself

nor another character, but the unspecified reader/viewer. Obviously, different kinds of motivation and tests of reliability are implied in these two character-narrations.

6. A number of contemporary reviewers, because they ignored or miscontrued the layered narrational structure in *Accident,* saw the film as an instance of classical narration. Judith Crist commented that "conventionally, then, with flashback, we are introduced to those [characters] involved with the girl and boy" (New York *World Journal Tribune,* April 18, 1967); Andrew Sarris asserts that the audience "is bored by the suppression of psychological investigation" (*Village Voice,* May 18, 1967); John Simon condemns Losey's "arty gimmicks" when he says, "There is the whole Francesca episode done in voice-over (action and off-screen dialogue deliberately unsynchronized) for no cogent reason" (*Film 67/68* 1968, 106–7).

Chapter 5

1. This brief summary is indebted to John Ward's *Alain Resnais, or the Theme of Time.* In his excellent discussion of Bergson's influence on Resnais, Ward notes that although Bergson was a prolific writer, he has confined his exposition of the philosopher's thought to "two of his more important books": *Time and Free Will* and *Matter and Memory* (1968, 5).

2. Scholes and David Bordwell both emphasize that film viewing is an active rather than passive enterprise for the viewer, and identify the determination of causality as basic to a viewer's activity in constructing a story from the data presented by the discourse. Scholes says: "Our primary effort in attending to a narration is to construct a satisfying order of events. To do this we must locate or provide two features: temporality and causality.... Above all, when we recognize a work as a story, we regard it as having a temporal sequentiality based upon cause and effect. This means that if the events in a story are presented in their temporal sequence, much of our narrativity ['the process by which a perceiver actively constructs a story from the fictional data provided by any narrative medium'] is devoted to establishing the causal connections between one event and the next. It means further that if the events themselves are presented out of a temporal sequence, we seek first to arrive at an understanding of the true temporal sequence in order to grasp the causal sequence informing the temporal" (1979, 422–3).

3. Both Losey and Pinter were attracted to this particular story for more than formal, aesthetic reasons. John Russell Taylor quoted Pinter describing his reaction to the Hartley novel: "I was reading it all at one sitting and, as it happened, alone in the house. And suddenly at a certain point near the climax of the story, I found myself in floods of tears. Really weeping. A few pages later I was off again. It was all very eerie. And when Joe asked if I would like to write a script based on the book my first thought was, impossible: I shall just be in tears for months at a time" (1970, 202).

Chapter 6

1. Richard Combs concluded that Lewis "characterises the [producer's] suggestion for a women's liberation slant as 'pretentious and derivative – and boring.' Later

Fielding roundly abuses a friend of his wife's who comes out with a phrase – 'woman is an occupied land.'... Thus the struggle of Elizabeth Fielding... to free herself from her husband's fantasies... is largely discarded as a subject too cliched to be worthy of attention" (1975, 143). It seems clear, however, that these scenes call into question Lewis's position rather than Elizabeth's, for they expose his discomfort and defensiveness about the very journey Elizabeth has embarked upon, whatever its outcome.

2. For a thorough exploration of the problematic treatment of women's desire, subjectivity, and economic status in Hollywood films, see Mary Ann Doane's *The Desire to Desire: The Woman's Film of the 1940s* (1987).

Filmography

1939
Pete Roleum and His Cousins
Producer, screenplay, director: Joseph Losey
Photography: Harold Muller
Animation: Charles Bowers
Puppets devised by: Howard Bay
Music: Hanns Eisler, Oscar Levant
Narrator: Hiram Sherman
Production company: Petroleum Industries Exhibition, Inc. for the New York World's Fair
Running time: 20 min.

1940
A Child Went Forth
Producers, directors: Joseph Losey, John Ferno
Screenplay: Joseph Losey, Munro Leaf
Photography: John Ferno
Music: Hanns Eisler
Narrator: Lloyd Gough
Production company: National Association of Nursery Educators
Running time: 18 min.

1941
Youth Gets a Break
Codirector, screenplay: Joseph Losey
Photography: John Ferno, Willard Van Dyke, Ralph Steiner
Production company: National Youth Administration
Running time: 20 min.

1945
A Gun in His Hand
Director: Joseph Losey

Screenplay: Charles Francis Royal, based on a story by Richard Landau
Photography: Jackson Rose
Music: Max Terr
Production company: MGM ("Crime Does Not Pay" series)
Cast: Anthony Caruso (Pinky), Richard Gaines (Inspector Dana), Ray Teal (O'Neill)
Running time: 19 min.

1948
The Boy with Green Hair
Producer: Stephen Ames
Director: Joseph Losey
Screenplay: Ben Barzman, Alfred Lewis Levitt, based on a story by Betty Beaton
Photography: George Barnes
Editor: Frank Doyle
Art directors: Albert D'Agostino, Ralph Berger
Music: Leigh Harline
Production company: RKO-Radio (a Dore Schary Presentation)
Cast: Dean Stockwell (Peter Frye), Pat O'Brien (Gramp), Robert Ryan (Dr. Evans),
Barbara Hale (Miss Brand), Walter Catlett (the King)
16mm: Films, Inc.
Video: Image Entertainment, Inc.
Running time: 82 min.

1950
The Lawless (British title: *The Dividing Line*)
Producers: William Pine, William Thomas
Director: Joseph Losey
Screenplay: Geoffrey Homes [Daniel Mainwaring], from his novel *The Voice of Stephen Wilder*
Photography: Roy Hunt
Editor: Howard Smith
Art director: Lewis H. Creber
Music: Mahlon Merrick
Production company: Paramount
Cast: MacDonald Carey (Larry Wilder), Gail Russell (Sunny Garcia), John Sands
(Joe Ferguson), Lalo Rios (Paul Rodriguez), Maurice Jara (Lopo Chavez)
Production time: 83 min.

1951
The Prowler
Producer: S. P. Eagle [Sam Spiegel]
Director: Joseph Losey
Screenplay: Dalton Trumbo, Hugo Butler, from an original story by Robert Thoeren,
Hans Wilhelm
Photography: Arthur Miller
Editor: Paul Weatherwax
Art director: Boris Leven

Music: Lyn Murray
Production company: Horizon Pictures
Cast: Van Heflin (Webb Garwood), Evelyn Keyes (Susan Gilvray), John Maxwell (Bud Crocker), Katherine Warren (Mrs. Crocker), Emerson Treacy (William Gilvray)
16mm: Ivy Films
Running time: 92 min.

1951
M
Producer: Seymour Nebenzal
Director: Joseph Losey
Screenplay: Norman Reilly Raine, Leo Katcher, from the original screenplay by Thea von Harbou, Fritz Lang
Photography: Ernest Lazlo
Editor: Edward Mann
Art director: Martin Obzina
Music: Michel Michelet
Production company: Columbia
Cast: David Wayne (Martin Harrow), Howard Da Silva (Carney), Luther Adler (Langley), Martin Gabel (Marshall), Steve Brodie (Lt. Baker), Raymond Burr (Pottsy)
Running time: 88 min.

1951
The Big Night
Producer: Philip A. Waxman
Director: Joseph Losey
Screenplay: Hugo Butler, Ring Lardner, Jr., Stanley Ellin, Joseph Losey, based on Ellin's novel *Dreadful Summit*
Photography: Hal Mohr
Editor: Edward Mann
Art director: Nicholas Remisoff
Music. Lyn Murray.
Production company: Philip Waxman, United Artists
Cast: John Barrymore, Jr. (Georgie La Main), Preston Foster (Andy La Main), Howland Chamberlin (Flanagan), Howard St. John (Al Judge), Dorothy Comingore (Julie Rostina)
16mm: Swank Motion Pictures
Running time: 75 min.

1952
Stranger on the Prowl (Italian title: *Imbarco a Mezzanotte;* British title: *Encounter*)
Producer: Noel Calef
Director: Andrea Forzano [Joseph Losey]
Screenplay: Andrea Forzano [Ben Barzman], based on a story by Calef
Photography: Henri Alekan
Editor: Thelma Connell
Art director: Antonio Valente

Music: G. C. Sonzogno
Production company: Consorzio Produttori Cinematografici Tirenia/Riviera Film, Inc.
Cast: Paul Muni (the Man), Joan Lorring (Angela), Vittorio Manunta (Giacomo Fontana)
Running time: 100 min. (United States and Britain, 82 min)

1954
The Sleeping Tiger
Producer: Victor Hanbury
Director: Victor Hanbury [Joseph Losey]
Screenplay: Derek Frye [Harold Buchman, Carl Foreman], based on the novel by Maurice Moiseiwitsch
Photography: Harry Waxman
Editor: Reginald Mills
Art director: John Stoll
Music: Malcolm Arnold
Production company: Insignia
Cast: Dirk Bogarde (Frank Clements), Alexis Smith (Glenda Esmond), Alexander Knox (Dr. Clive Esmond), Hugh Griffith (Inspector Simmons)
Running time: 89 min.

1955
A Man on the Beach
Producer: Anthony Hinds
Director: Joseph Losey
Screenplay: Jimmy Sangster, based on a story, "Chance at the Wheel," by Victor Canning
Photography: Wilkie Cooper
Editor: Henry Richardson
Art director: Edward Marshall
Music: John Hotchkis
Production company: Hammer Films
Cast: Donald Wolfit (Carter), Michael Medwin (Max), Michael Ripper (chauffeur), Alex de Gallier (casino manager)
Running time: 29 min.

1956
The Intimate Stranger (U.S. title: *Finger of Guilt*)
Producer: Alec C. Snowden
Director: Joseph Walton (British credit), Alec Snowden (U.S. credit) [Joseph Losey]
Screenplay: Peter Howard [Howard Koch]
Photography: Gerald Gibbs
Editor: Geoffrey Muller
Art director: Wilfred Arnold
Music: Trevor Duncan.
Production company: Anglo Guild

Cast: Richard Basehart (Reggie Wilson), Mary Murphy (Evelyn Stewart), Constance Cummings (Kay Wallace), Roger Livesey (Ben Case), Mervyn Johns (Ernest Chaple)
16mm: Kit Parker Films
Running time: 95 min. (United States, 71 min.)

1957
Time Without Pity
Producers: John Arnold, Anthony Simmons
Director: Joseph Losey
Screenplay: Ben Barzman, based on the play *Someone Waiting* by Emlyn Williams
Photography: Freddie Francis
Editor: Alan Osbiston
Art director: Bernard Sarron
Music: Tristram Cary
Production company: Harlequin
Cast: Michael Redgrave (David Graham), Ann Todd (Honor Stanford), Leo McKern (Robert Stanford), Peter Cushing (Jeremy Clayton), Alec McCowen (Alec Graham), Joan Plowright (Agnes Cole)
16mm: Kit Parker Films
Running time: 88 min.

1958
The Gypsy and the Gentleman
Producer: Maurice Cowan
Director: Joseph Losey
Screenplay: Janet Green, based on the novel *Darkness I Leave You* by Nina Warner Hooke
Photography: Jack Hildyard
Editor: Reginald Beck
Art director: Ralph Brinton
Music: Hans May
Production company: Rank
Cast: Melina Mercouri (Belle), Keith Michell (Sir Paul Deverill), Patrick McGoohan (Jess), Flora Robson (Mrs. Haggard)
Running time: 107 min. (United States, 90 min.)

1959
Blind Date (U.S. title: *Chance Meeting*)
Producer: David Deutsch
Director: Joseph Losey
Screenplay: Ben Barzman, Millard Lampell, based on the novel by Leigh Howard
Photography: Christopher Challis
Editor: Reginald Mills
Art director: Harry Pottle
Music: Richard Rodney Bennett
Production company: Independent Artists (a Julian Wintle–Leslie Parkyn Production)

Cast: Hardy Kruger (Jan Van Rooyen), Stanley Baker (Inspector Morgan), Micheline Presle (Lady Fenton, called Jacqueline Cousteau), Robert Flemyng (Sir Brian Lewis), Gordon Jackson (Police Sergeant)
Running time: 95 min.

1960
The Criminal (U.S. title: *The Concrete Jungle*)
Producer: Jack Greenwood
Director: Joseph Losey
Screenplay: Alun Owen, based on an original story by Jimmy Sangster
Photography: Robert Krasker
Editor: Reginald Mills
Art director: Scott Macgregor
Music: Johnny Dankworth
Production company: Merton Parke Studios
Cast: Stanley Baker (Johnny Bannion), Sam Wanamaker (Mike Carter), Margit Saad (Suzanne), Patrick Magee (Chief Warder Barrowes), Gregoire Aslan (Frank Saffron), Jill Bennett (Maggie)
16mm: Corinth Films
Running time: 97 min. (United States, 86 min.)

1962
Eve
Producers: Robert Hakim, Raymond Hakim
Director: Joseph Losey
Screenplay: Hugo Butler, Evan Jones, based on the novel by James Hadley Chase
Photography: Gianni Di Venanzo
Editors: Reginald Beck, Franca Silvi
Art directors: Richard MacDonald, Luigi Scaccianoce
Music: Michel Legrand
Production company: Paris Film/Interopa Film – Rome
Cast: Jeanne Moreau (Eve Olivier), Stanley Baker (Tyvian Jones), Virna Lisi (Francesca Ferrara), James Villiers (Arthur McCormick)
Running time: France: 100 min.; United States: 115 min.; originally 155 min., subsequently cut by Losey to 135 min.

1963
The Damned (U.S. title: *These Are the Damned* [1965])
Producer: Anthony Hinds
Director: Joseph Losey
Screenplay: Evan Jones, based on the novel *The Children of Light* by H. L. Lawrence
Photography: Arthur Grant
Editor: Reginald Mills
Art director: Don Mingaye
Music: James Bernard
Production company: Hammer/Swallow
Cast: MacDonald Carey (Simon Wells), Shirley Ann Field (Joan), Viveca Lindfors

(Freya Neilson), Alexander Knox (Bernard), Oliver Reed (King), James Villiers (Captain Gregory)
16mm: Kit Parker Films; Swank Motion Pictures
Running time: 87 min. (United States: 77 min.)

1963
The Servant
Producers: Joseph Losey, Norman Priggen
Director: Joseph Losey
Screenplay: Harold Pinter, based on the novel by Robin Maugham
Photography: Douglas Slocombe
Editor: Reginald Mills
Production designer: Richard MacDonald
Art Director: Ted Clements
Music: John Dankworth
Production company: Springbok/Elstree
Cast: Dirk Bogarde (Hugo Barrett), James Fox (Tony), Wendy Craig (Susan), Sarah Miles (Vera)
16mm: Films, Inc.
Video: HBO Video
Running time: 115 min.

1964
King and Country
Producers: Joseph Losey, Norman Priggen
Director: Joseph Losey
Screenplay: Evan Jones, from the play *Hamp* by John Wilson, based on a story by James Lansdale Hodson
Photography: Denys Coop
Editor: Reginald Mills
Design consultant: Richard MacDonald
Art director: Peter Mullins
Music: Larry Adler
Production company: B.H.E. Productions
Cast: Dirk Bogarde (Capt. Hargreaves), Tom Courtenay (Pvt. Hamp), Leo McKern (Capt. O'Sullivan), Barry Foster (Lt. Webb), James Villiers (Capt. Midgley), Peter Copley (Colonel), Vivian Matalon (Padre), Jeremy Spenser (Pvt. Sparrow)
16mm: Films, Inc.; Ivy Films
Running time: 86 min.

1966
Modesty Blaise
Producer: Joseph Janni
Director: Joseph Losey
Screenplay: Evan Jones, based on the comic strip created by Peter O'Donnell and Jim Holdaway
Photography: Jack Hildyard

Editor: Reginald Beck
Production designer: Richard MacDonald
Music: John Dankworth
Production company: Modesty Blaise, Ltd.
Cast: Monica Vitti (Modesty), Terence Stamp (Willie Garvin), Dirk Bogarde (Gabriel), Harry Andrews (Sir Gerald Tarrant)
Running time: 119 min.

1967
Accident
Producers: Joseph Losey, Norman Priggen
Director: Joseph Losey
Screenplay: Harold Pinter, based on the novel by Nicholas Mosley
Photography: Gerry Fisher
Editor: Reginald Beck
Art director: Carmen Dillon
Music: John Dankworth
Production company: Royal Avenue Chelsea
Cast: Dirk Bogarde (Stephen), Stanley Baker (Charley), Jacqueline Sassard (Anna), Michael York (William), Vivien Merchant (Rosalind), Delphine Seyrig (Francesca), Alexander Knox (Provost), Ann Firbank (Laura), Harold Pinter (Mr. Bell), Nicholas Mosley (a don)
16mm: Films, Inc.
Video: HBO Video
Running time: 105 min.

1968
Boom!
Producers: John Heyman, Norman Priggen
Director: Joseph Losey
Screenplay: Tennessee Williams, based on his play *The Milk Train Doesn't Stop Here Anymore*
Photography: Douglas Slocombe
Editor: Reginald Beck
Art director: Richard MacDonald
Music: John Barry
Production company: World Film Services/Moon Lake Productions
Cast: Elizabeth Taylor (Flora Goforth), Richard Burton (Chris Flanders), Noel Coward (Witch of Capri), Joanna Shimkus (Blackie), Michael Dunn (Rudy)
16mm: Swank Motion Pictures
Running time: 110 min.

1968
Secret Ceremony
Producers: John Heyman, Norman Priggen
Director: Joseph Losey
Screenplay: George Tabori, from a novel by Marco Denevi

Photography: Gerry Fisher
Editor: Reginald Beck
Production designer: Richard MacDonald
Art director: John Clark
Music: Richard Rodney Bennett
Production company: World Film Services/Universal Pictures
Cast: Elizabeth Taylor (Leonora), Mia Farrow (Cenci), Robert Mitchum (Albert), Peggy Ashcroft (Hannah), Pamela Brown (Hilda)
16mm: Swank Motion Pictures
Video: KVC Videos
Running time: 109 min.

1970
Figures in a Landscape
Producer: John Kohn
Director: Joseph Losey
Screenplay: Robert Shaw, based on a novel by Barry England
Photography: Henri Alekan
Editor: Reginald Beck
Art director: Ted Tester
Music: Richard Rodney Bennett
Production company: Cinema Center Films
Cast: Robert Shaw (MacConnachie), Malcolm McDowell (Ansell)
16mm: Kit Parker Films
Running time: 109 min.

1971
The Go-Between
Producers: John Heyman, Norman Priggen
Director: Joseph Losey
Screenplay: Harold Pinter, based on the novel by L. P. Hartley
Photography: Gerry Fisher
Editor: Reginald Beck
Art director: Carmen Dillon
Music: Michel Legrand
Production company: EMI/World Film Services
Cast: Julie Christie (Marian Maudsley), Alan Bates (Ted Burgess), Dominic Guard (Leo Colston as a boy), Michael Redgrave (Leo as a man), Margaret Leighton (Mrs. Maudsley), Michael Gough (Mr. Maudsley), Edward Fox (Hugh Trimingham), Richard Gibson (Marcus)
16mm: Films, Inc.; Swank Motion Pictures
Running time: 116 min.

1972
The Assassination of Trotsky
Producers: Joseph Losey, Norman Priggen
Director: Joseph Losey

Screenplay: Nicholas Mosley, Masolino d'Amico
Photography: Pasquale de Santis
Editor: Reginald Beck
Production designer: Richard MacDonald
Art director: Arrigo Equini
Music: Egisto Macchi
Production company: Cinetel/Dino de Laurentiis
Cast: Richard Burton (Leon Trotsky), Alain Delon (Frank Jacson), Romy Schneider (Gita), Valentina Cortese (Natalya)
Video: Facets Video; Republic Pictures Home Video
Running time: 103 min.

1973
A Doll's House
Producer: Joseph Losey
Director: Joseph Losey
Screenplay: David Mercer, based on the play by Henrik Ibsen, translated into English by Michael Meyer
Photography: Gerry Fisher
Editor: Reginald Beck
Art director: Eileen Diss
Music: Michel Legrand
Production company: World Film Services (shown in U.S. on ABC-TV)
Cast: Jane Fonda (Nora), David Warner (Torvald), Trevor Howard (Dr. Rank), Delphine Seyrig (Kristine Linde), Edward Fox (Nils Krogstad)
16mm: Kit Parker Films; Swank Motion Pictures
Video: Prism Entertainment
Running time: 106 min.

1974
Galileo
Producer: Ely Landau
Director: Joseph Losey
Screenplay: Barbara Bray and Joseph Losey, from the play *Life of Galileo* by Bertolt Brecht, translated into English by Charles Laughton
Photography: Michael Reed
Editor: Reginald Beck
Production designer: Richard MacDonald
Music: Hans Eisler
Production company: Ely Landau Organization
Cast: Topol (Galileo Galilei), Edward Fox (Cardinal Inquisitor), Colin Blakeley (Priuli), Clive Revill (ballad singer), Georgia Brown (ballad singer's wife), Margaret Leighton (court lady), John Gielgud (old cardinal), Michael Gough (Sagredo), Michel Lonsdale (Cardinal Barberini/Pope)
Running time: 145 min.

1975
The Romantic Englishwoman
Producer: Daniel M. Angel
Director: Joseph Losey
Screenplay: Tom Stoppard, Thomas Wiseman, based on Wiseman's novel
Photography: Gerry Fisher
Editor: Reginald Beck
Art director: Richard MacDonald
Music: Richard Hartley
Production company: Dial Films/Meric Matalon
Cast: Glenda Jackson (Elizabeth Fielding), Michael Caine (Lewis Fielding), Helmut Berger (Thomas Hursa), Kate Nelligan (Isabel), Rene Kolldehof (Herman), Michel Lonsdale (Swan)
Video: Warner Home Video
Running time: 116 min.

1976
Mr. Klein
Producers: Raymond Danon, Alain Delon
Director: Joseph Losey
Screenplay: Franco Solinas
Photography: Gerry Fisher
Editor: Henri Lanoë
Art director: Alexandre Trauner
Music: Egisto Macchi, Pierre Porte
Production company: Basil Films
Cast: Alain Delon (Robert Klein), Jeanne Moreau (Florence), Suzanne Flon (concierge), Michel Lonsdale (Pierre), Juliet Berto (Janine)
Video: RCA/Columbia Pictures Home Video
Running time: 122 min.

1978
Les Routes du Sud
Producer: Yves Rousset-Rouard
Director: Joseph Losey
Screenplay: Jorge Semprun
Photography: Gerry Fisher
Editor: Reginald Beck
Art director: Alexandre Trauner
Music: Michel Legrand
Production company: Société française de production, Tinacra Films, FR 3 [Paris]/Profilmes [Barcelona]
Cast: Yves Montand (Jean Larrea), Miou Miou (Julia), Laurent Malet (Laurent Larrea)
Video: Connoisseur Video Collection
Running time: 97 min.

1979
Don Giovanni
Producers: Luciano De Feo, Michel Seydoux, Robert Nador
Director: Joseph Losey
Screenplay: Mozart's opera *Don Giovanni* with libretto by Lorenzo Da Ponte
Adaptation: Joseph Losey, Patricia Losey, Frantz Salieri
Photography: Gerry Fisher, Carlo Poletti
Editors: Reginald Beck, Emma Menenti, Marie Castro Vazquez
Art director: Alexandre Trauner
Music: Mozart, performed by the Orchestra and Chorus of the Paris Opera, directed by Lorin Maazel
Production company: Opera Film Produzione [Rome]; Gaumont/Camera One/Antenna-2 [Paris]; Janus Films [Frankfurt]
Cast: Ruggero Raimondi (Don Giovanni), John Macurdy (commendatore), Edda Moser (Donna Anna), Kiri te Kanawa (Donna Elvira)
16mm: New Yorker Films
Running time: 176 min.

1982
La Truite
Producer: Yves Rousset-Rouard
Director: Joseph Losey
Screenplay: Joseph Losey, Monique Lange, based on the novel by Roger Vailland
Photography: Henri Alekan
Editor: Marie Castro Vazquez
Art director: Alexandre Trauner
Music: Richard Hartley
Production company: Gaumont-TF1-SFPC
Cast: Isabelle Huppert (Frédérique), Jean-Pierre Cassel (Rampert), Jeanne Moreau (Lou), Jacques Spiesser (Galuchat), Isao Yamagata (Daigo)
Video: RCA/Columbia Pictures Home Video
Running time: 105 min.

1985
Steaming
Producer: Paul Mills
Director: Joseph Losey
Screenplay: Patricia Losey, based on the play by Nell Dunn
Photography: Christopher Challis
Art director: Michael Pickwoad
Production company: Columbia
Cast: Vanessa Redgrave (Nancy), Sarah Miles (Sarah), Dianna Dors (Violet), Patti Love (Josie)
Video: New World Video
Running time: 95 min.

All Quiet on the Western Front, dir. Lewis Milestone (Universal, USA, 1930)

All Quiet on the Western Front, dir. Delbert Mann (Norman Rosemont Productions, USA, 1979)

Breaker Morant, dir. Bruce Beresford (Australia, 1979)

Charade, dir. Stanley Donen (Universal, USA, 1963)

Discreet Charm of the Bourgeoisie, The, dir. Luis Bunuel (France, 1972)

Double Indemnity, dir. Billy Wilder (Paramount, USA, 1944)

Execution of Private Slovik, The, dir. Lamont Johnson (Universal, USA, 1974)

400 Blows, The (Les quatre cents coups), dir. François Truffaut (France, 1959)

Hiroshima mon amour, dir. Alain Resnais (France, 1959)

How Many Miles to Babylon? dir. Moira Armstrong (Great Britain, 1982)

Jane Eyre, dir. Robert Stevenson (Twentieth Century-Fox, USA, 1944)

La guerre est finie, dir. Alain Resnais (France, 1966)

Mother, dir. V. I. Pudovkin (USSR, 1926)

Now, Voyager, dir. Irving Rapper (Warners, USA, 1942)

Paths of Glory, dir. Stanley Kubrick (United Artists, USA, 1957)

Rack, The, dir. Arnold Lavin (Metro-Goldwyn-Mayer, USA, 1956)

Saturday Night and Sunday Morning, dir. Karel Reisz (Great Britain, 1961)

To Catch a Thief, dir. Alfred Hitchcock (Paramount, USA, 1954)

Works Cited

Becker, Ernest. *The Denial of Death.* New York: The Free Press, 1973.

Black, David Alan. "Genette and Film: Narrative Level in the Fiction Cinema." *Wide Angle* 8, nos. 3–4 (1986): 19–26.

Bonitzer, Pascal. "Here: The Notion of the Shot and Subject in Cinema." *Film Reader* 4 (1979): 108–19.

Bordwell, David. *Narration in the Fiction Film.* Madison: University of Wisconsin Press, 1985.

Bourne, J. M. *Britain and the Great War, 1914–1918.* London: Arnold, 1989.

Branigan, Edward R. *Point of View in the Cinema: A Theory of Narration and Subjectivity in Classical Film.* Berlin: Mouton Publishers, 1984.

"Point of View in the Fiction Film." *Wide Angle* 8, nos. 3–4 (1986): 4–7.

Bresson, Robert. *Notes on Cinematography.* New York: Urizen, 1977.

Browne, Nick. *The Rhetoric of Filmic Narration.* Ann Arbor: UMI Research Press, 1982.

"Introduction." *Film Reader* 4 (1979): 105–7.

Campbell, Joseph. *The Hero with a Thousand Faces.* 2d ed. Bollingen Series XVII. Princeton, N.J.: Princeton University Press, 1968.

Chatman, Seymour. Review of *Narration in the Fiction Film. Wide Angle* 8, nos. 3–4 (1986): 139–41.

Story and Discourse: Narrative Structure in Fiction and Film. Ithaca, N.Y.: Cornell University Press, 1978.

Ciment, Michel. *Conversations with Losey.* London: Methuen, 1985.

Combs, Richard. "Losey, *Galileo* and *The Romantic Englishwoman.*" *Sight and Sound* 44 (Summer 1975): 139–43.

Doane, Mary Ann. *The Desire to Desire: The Woman's Film of the 1940s.* Bloomington: Indiana University Press, 1987.

Fussell, Paul. *The Great War and Modern Memory.* Oxford University Press, 1977.

Genette, Gerard. *Narrative Discourse: An Essay in Method.* Trans. Jane E. Lewin. Ithaca, N.Y.: Cornell University Press, 1980.

Gill, Brendan. Review of *King and Country,* by Joseph Losey. *New Yorker,* 5 February 1966, p. 124.

Gow, Gordon. "Weapons: Joseph Losey in an Interview with Gordon Gow." *Films and Filming* 18, no. 1 (October 1971): 37–41.

Gussow, Mel. "A Conversation (Pause): From an Interview with Harold Pinter." *Performing Arts* 6 (June 1972): 25–6.

Hartley, L. P. *The Go-Between*. New York: Stein & Day, 1984.

Henderson, Brian. "Tense, Mood, and Voice in Film: Notes after Genette." *Film Quarterly* 36 (Summer 1983): 4–7.

Hirsch, Foster. *Joseph Losey*. Boston: Twayne, 1980.

Housman, A. E. *More Poems*. New York: Knopf, 1936.

Houston, Beverle, and Marsha Kinder. "The Losey–Pinter Collaboration." *Film Quarterly* 32 (Fall 1978): 17–30.

Jacob, Gilles. "Joseph Losey, or the Camera Calls." *Sight and Sound* 35 (Spring 1966): 62–7.

Kawin, Bruce. *Mindscreen: Bergman, Godard, and First-Person Film*. Princeton, N.J.: Princeton University Press, 1978.

"An Outline of Film Voices." *Film Quarterly* 38 (Winter 1984): 38–46.

Klein, Joanne. *Making Pictures: The Pinter Screenplays*. Columbus: Ohio State University Press, 1985.

Kozloff, Sarah. *Invisible Storytellers: Voice-Over Narration in American Fiction Film*. Berkeley & Los Angeles: University of California Press, 1988.

Review of *Narration in the Fiction Film*. *Film Quarterly* 40 (Fall 1986): 43–5.

Leahy, James. *The Cinema of Joseph Losey*. New York: Barnes, 1967.

Losey, Joseph. "Dialogue on Film." *American Film* 6 (November 1980): 53–60.

"Speak, Think, Stand Up." *Film Culture* 50–1 (Fall & Winter 1970): 53–61.

Maugham, Robin. *The Servant*. New York: Avon, 1964.

Milne, Tom, ed. *Losey on Losey*. Garden City, N.Y.: Doubleday, 1968.

Mosley, Nicholas. *Accident*. New York: New American Library, 1967.

Navasky, Victor. *Naming Names*. New York: Penguin, 1980.

Phillips, Gene D. "Hollywood Exile: An Interview with Joseph Losey." *Journal of Popular Film* 5, no. 1 (1976): 29–35.

Pinter, Harold. *Five Screenplays*. London: Methuen, 1971.

Pipolo, Tony. "The Aptness of Terminology: Point of View, Consciousness, and *Letter from an Unknown Woman*." *Film Reader* 4 (1979): 166–79.

Rush, Jeffrey S. "Lyric Oneness: The Free Syntactical Indirect and the Boundary Between Narrative and Narration." *Wide Angle* 8, nos. 3–4 (1986): 27–33.

Scholes, Robert. "Narration and Narrativity in Film." In *Film Theory and Criticism* 2d ed., edited by Gerald Mast and Marshall Cohen, 417–33. Oxford University Press, 1979.

Simon, William. "An Approach to Point of View." *Film Reader* 4 (1979): 145–51.

Taylor, John Russell. *"Accident." Sight and Sound* 35 (Autumn 1966): 179–84.

"Dateline: Report on *The Go-Between*." *Sight and Sound* 39 (Autumn 1970): 202–3.

Tomasulo, Frank P. "Narrate and Describe?: Point of View in *Citizen Kane*'s Thatcher Sequence." *Wide Angle* 8 nos. 3–4 (1986): 45–52.

Walker, Alexander. *Hollywood U.K.: The British Film Industry in the Sixties*. New York: Stein & Day, 1974.

Ward, John. *Alain Resnais, or the Theme of Time*. Garden City, N.Y.: Doubleday, 1968.

Wilson, George M. *Narration in Light: Studies in Cinematic Point of View*. Baltimore: Johns Hopkins University Press, 1986.

Wiseman, Thomas. *The Romantic Englishwoman*. New York: Putnam, 1972.

Young, Vernon. *On Film: Unpopular Essays on a Popular Art*. New York: Quadrangle, 1972.

Index

173